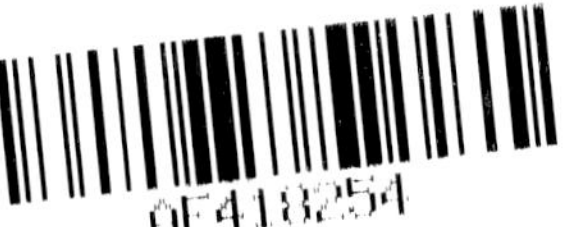

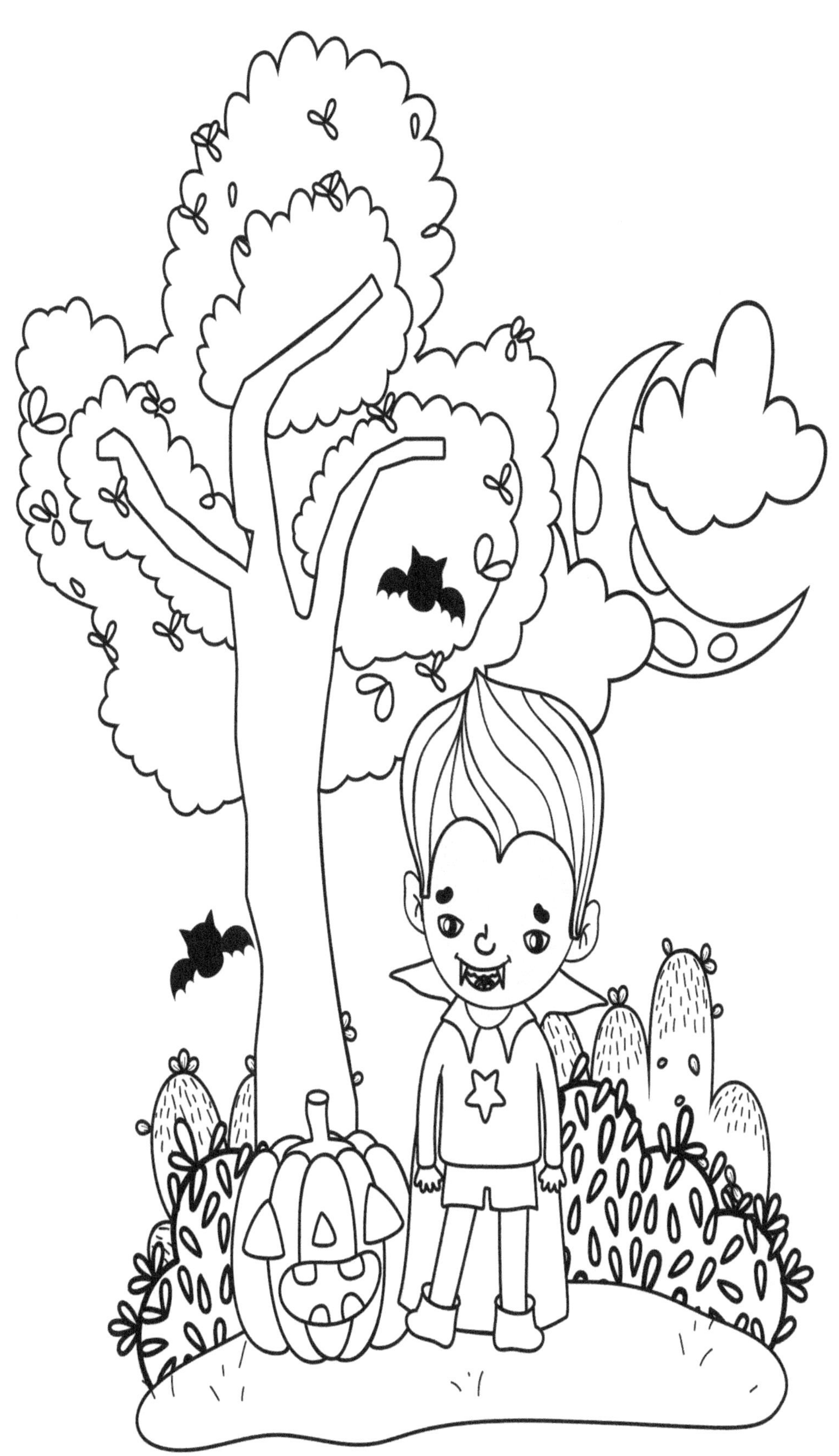

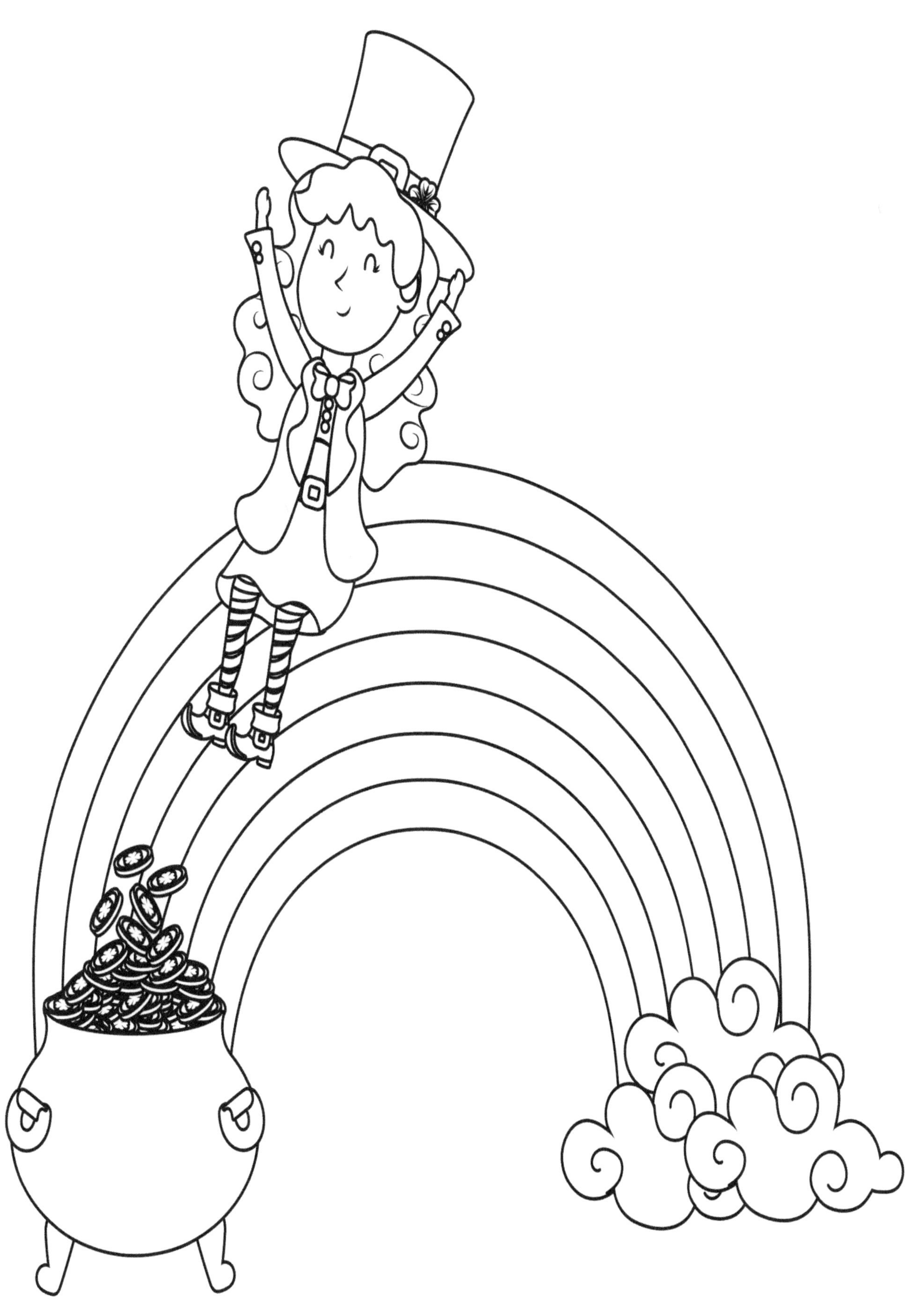

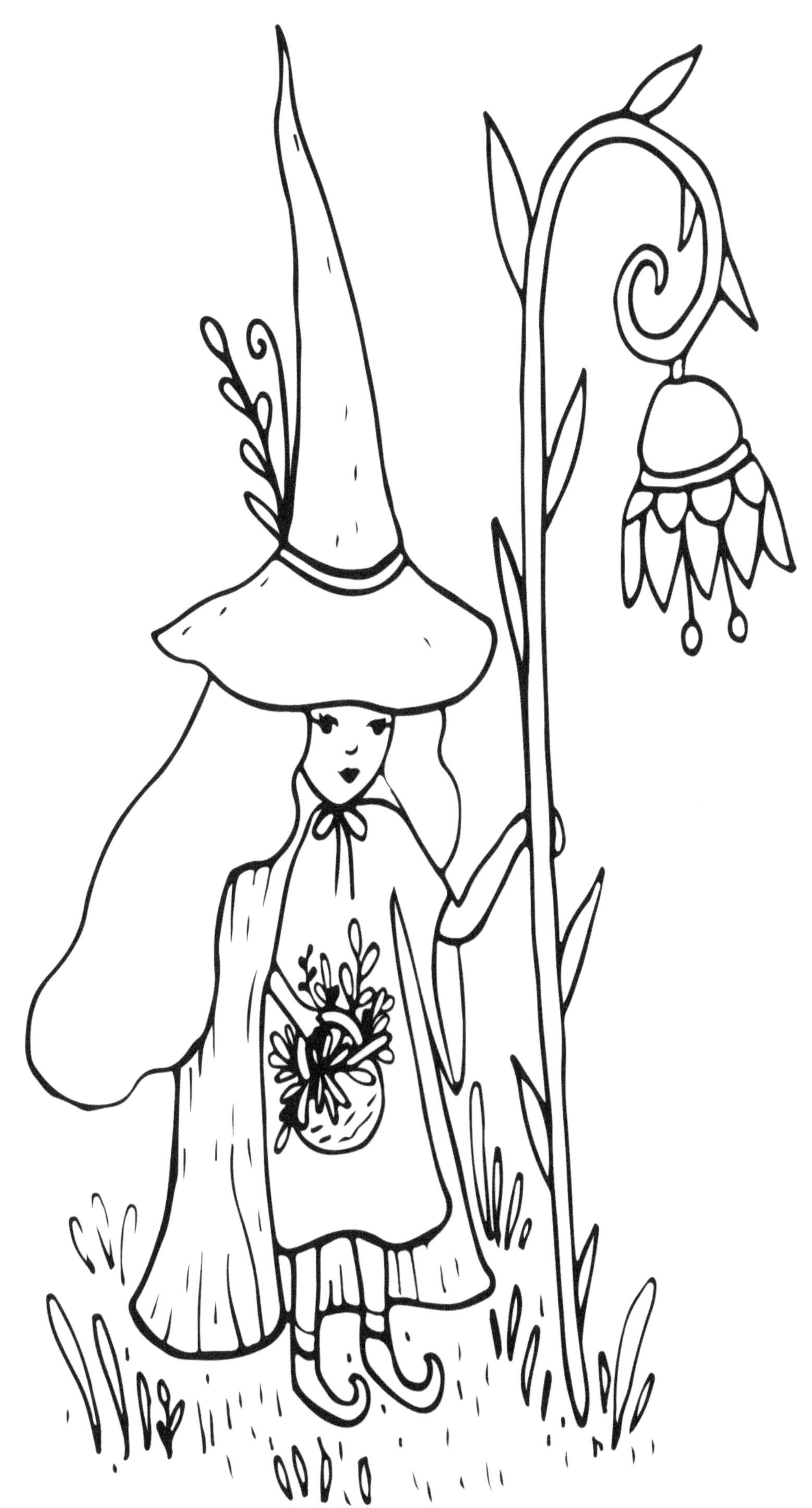

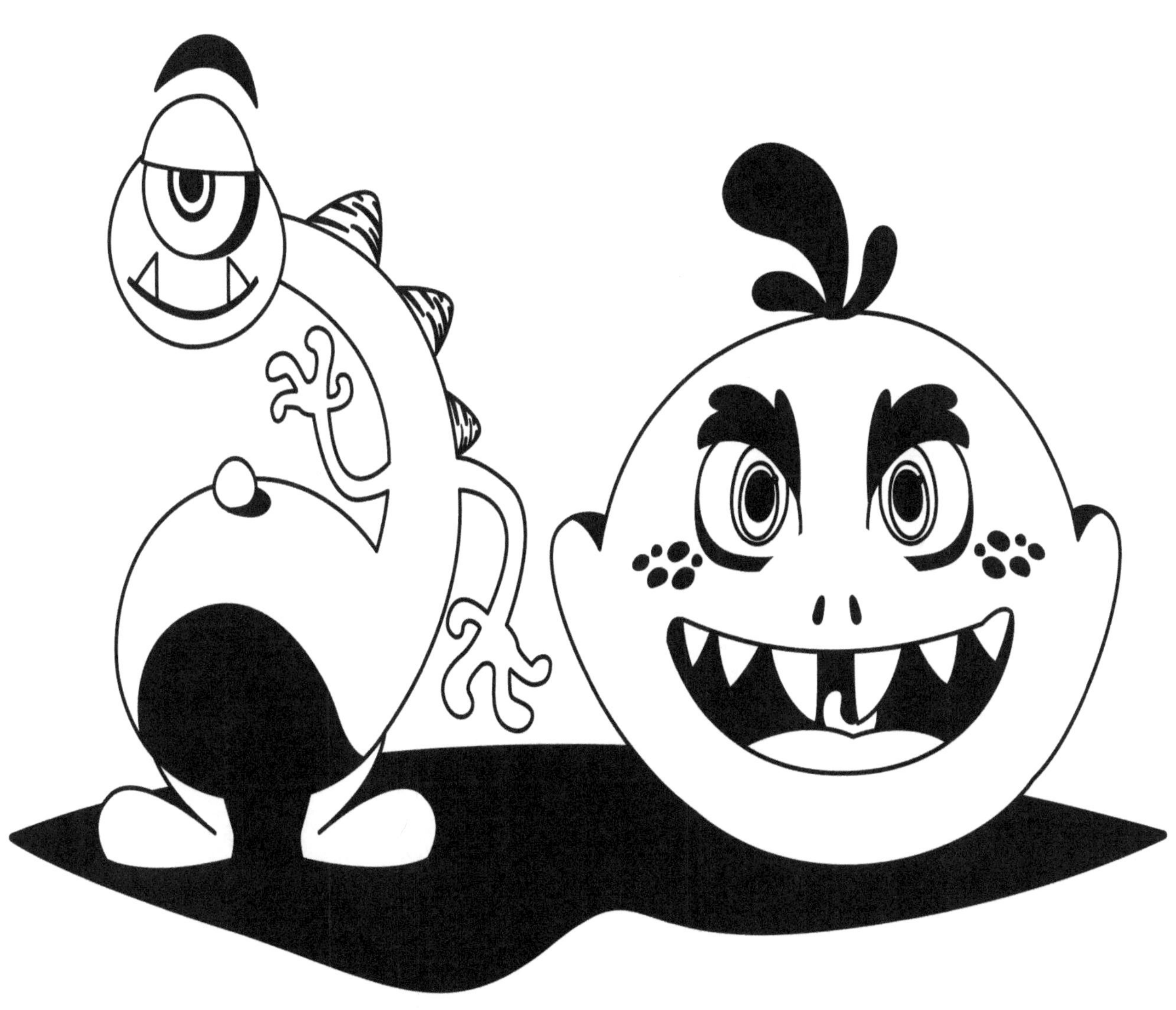

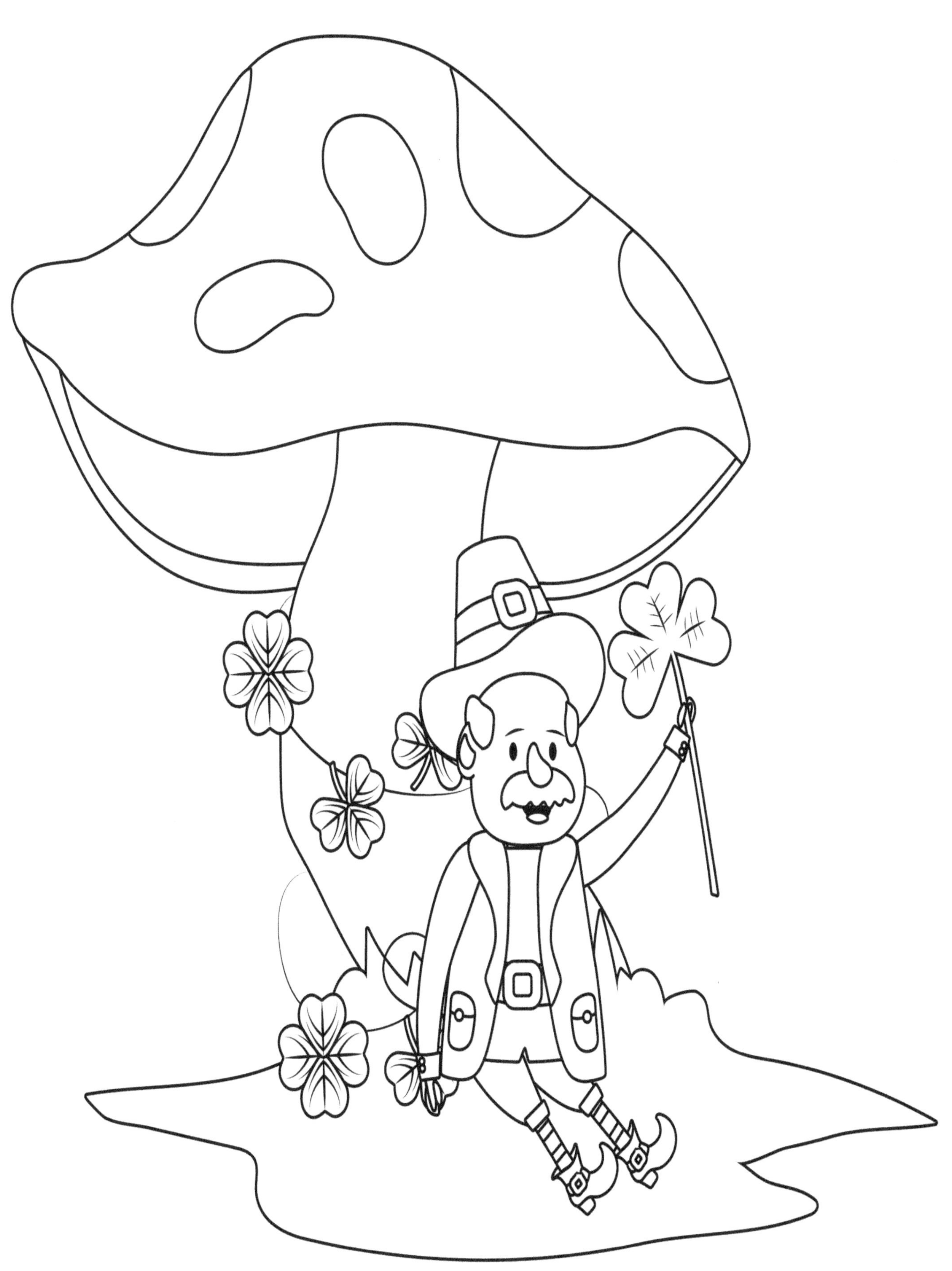

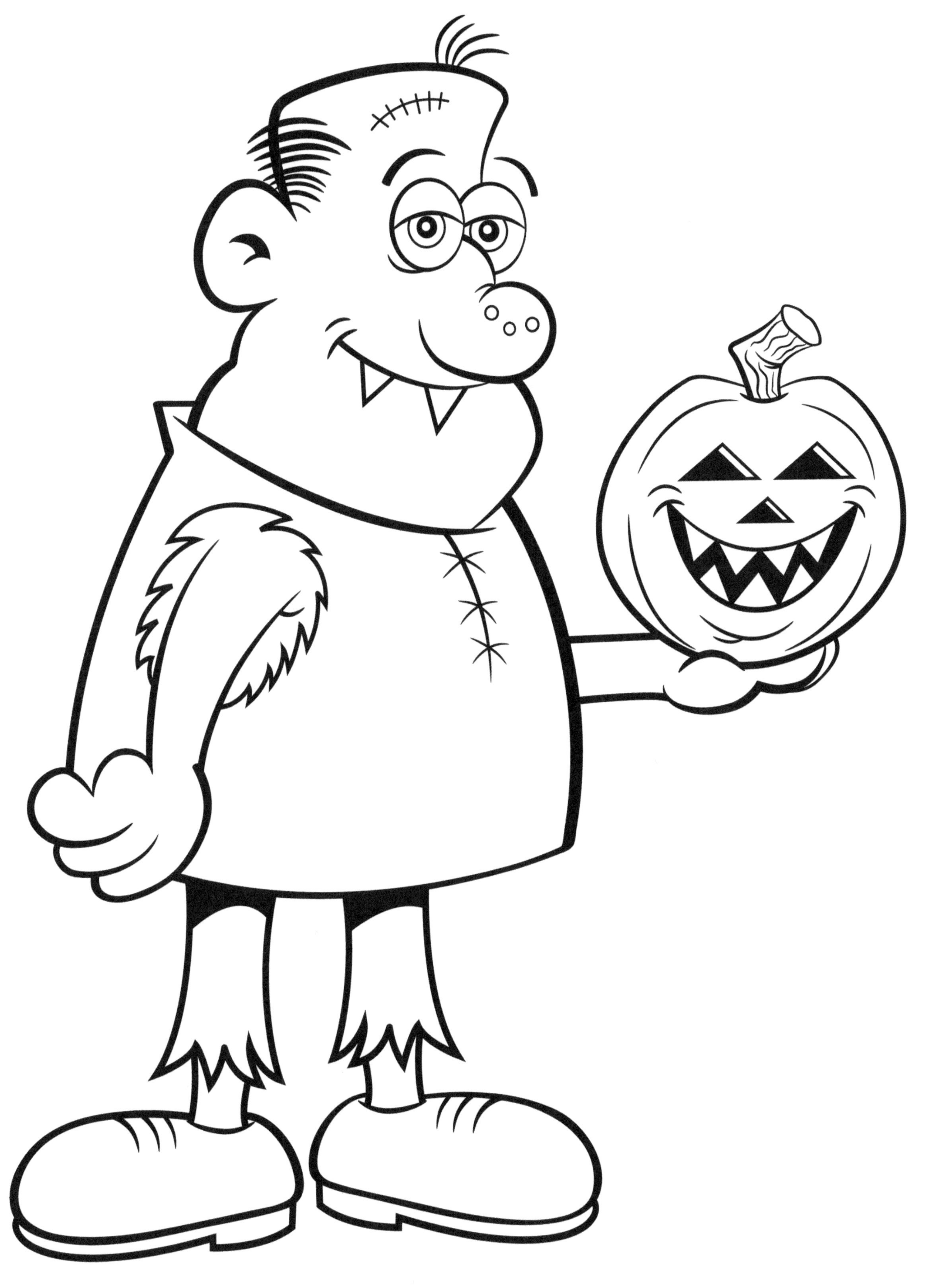

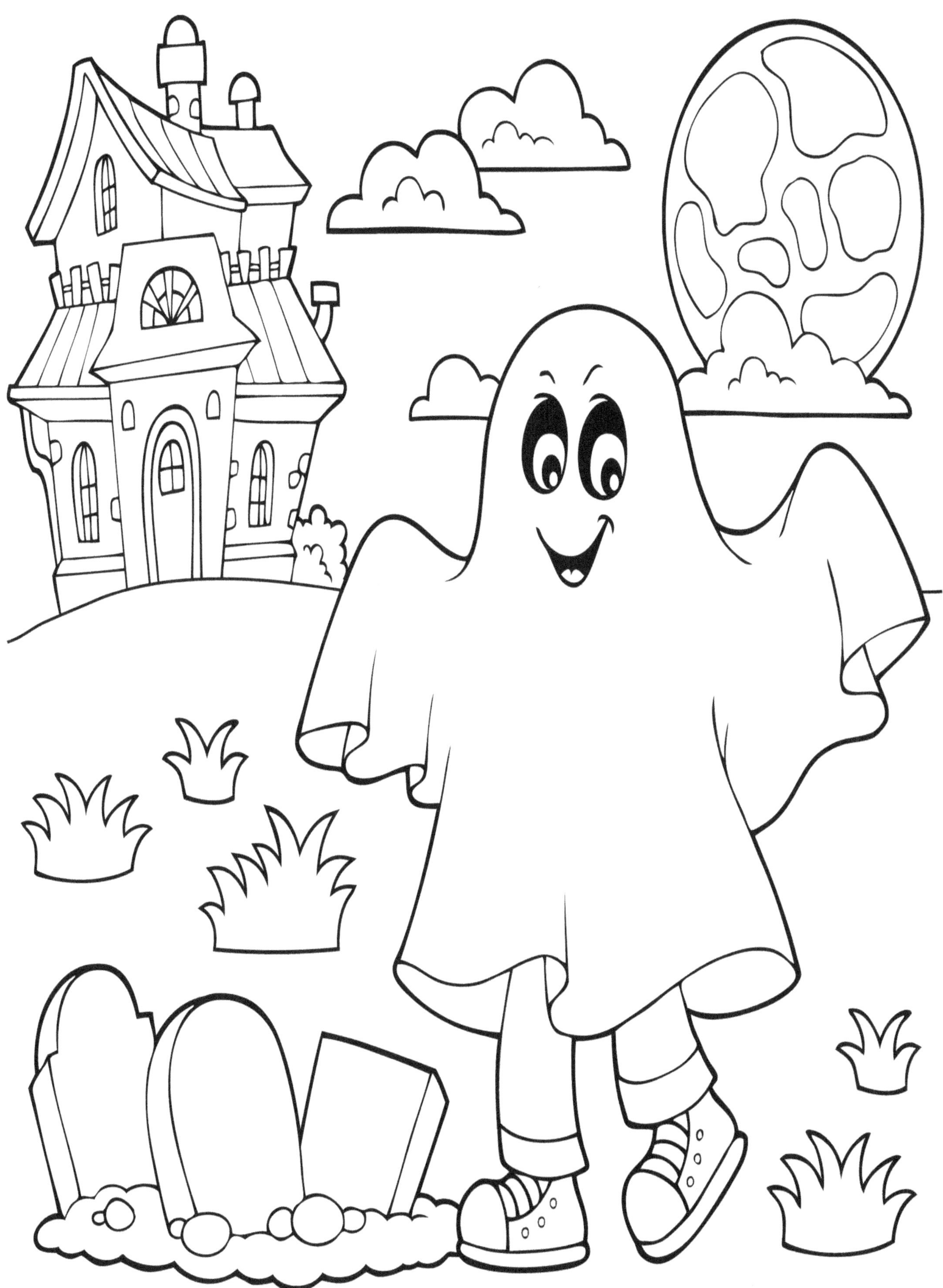

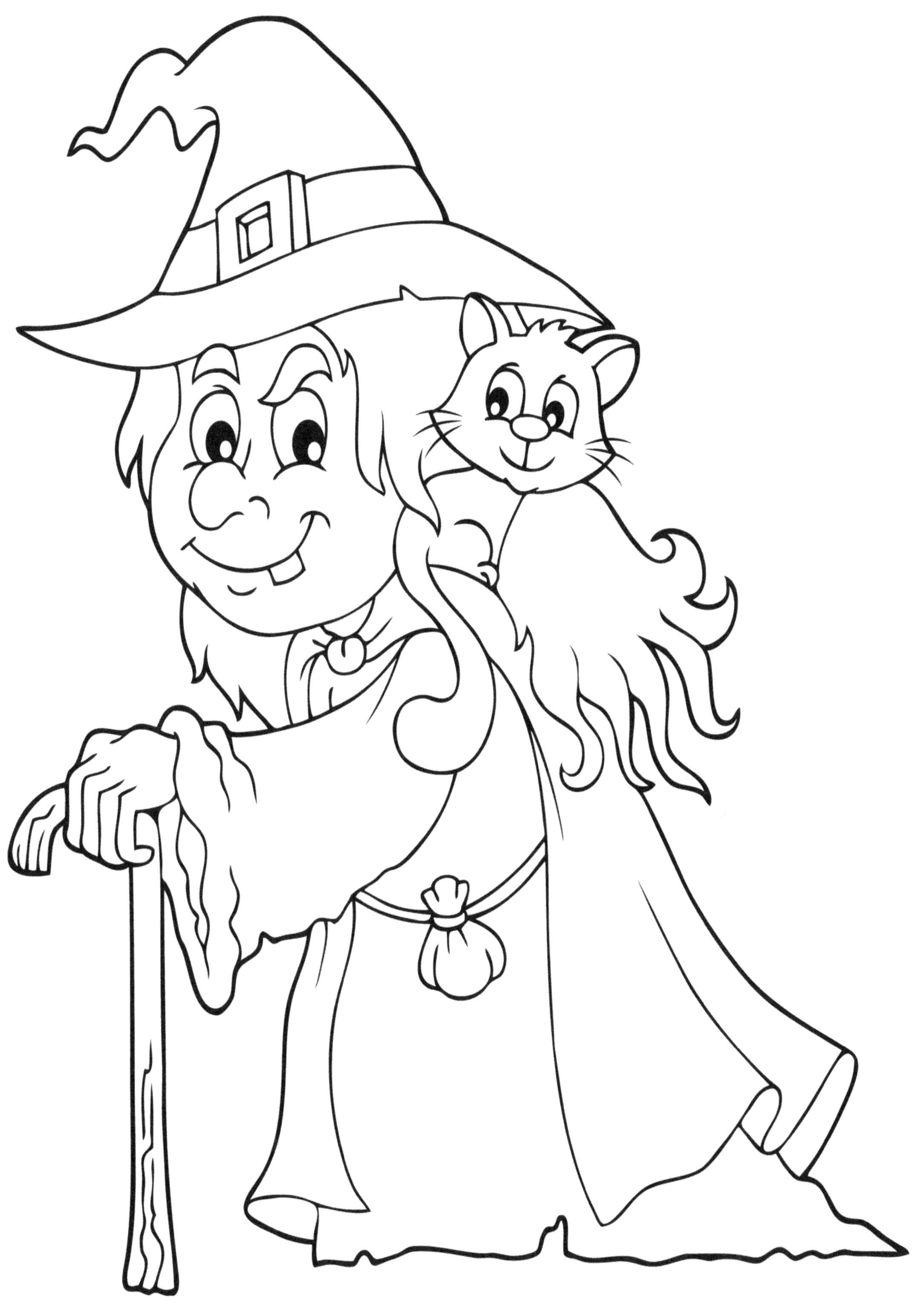

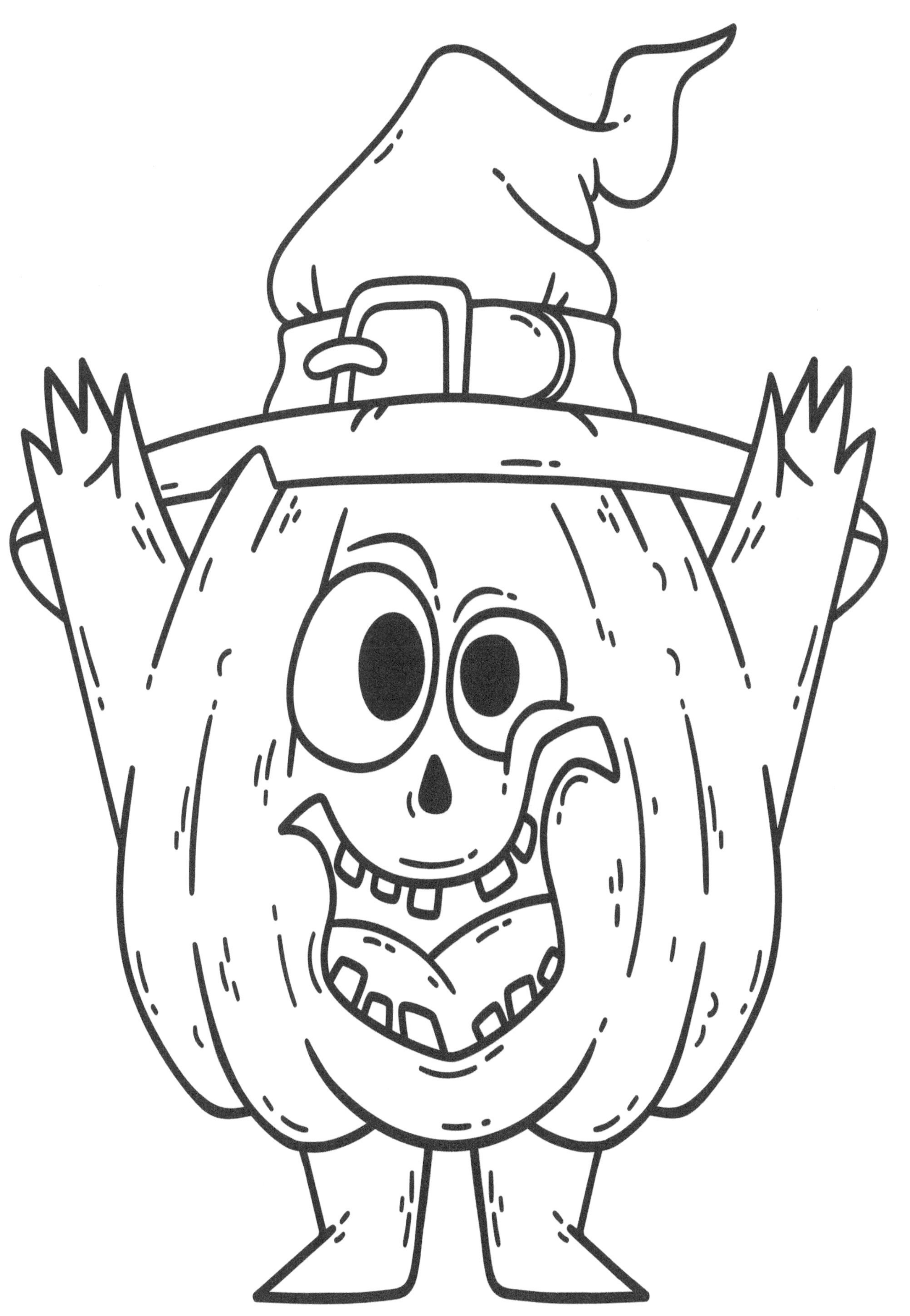

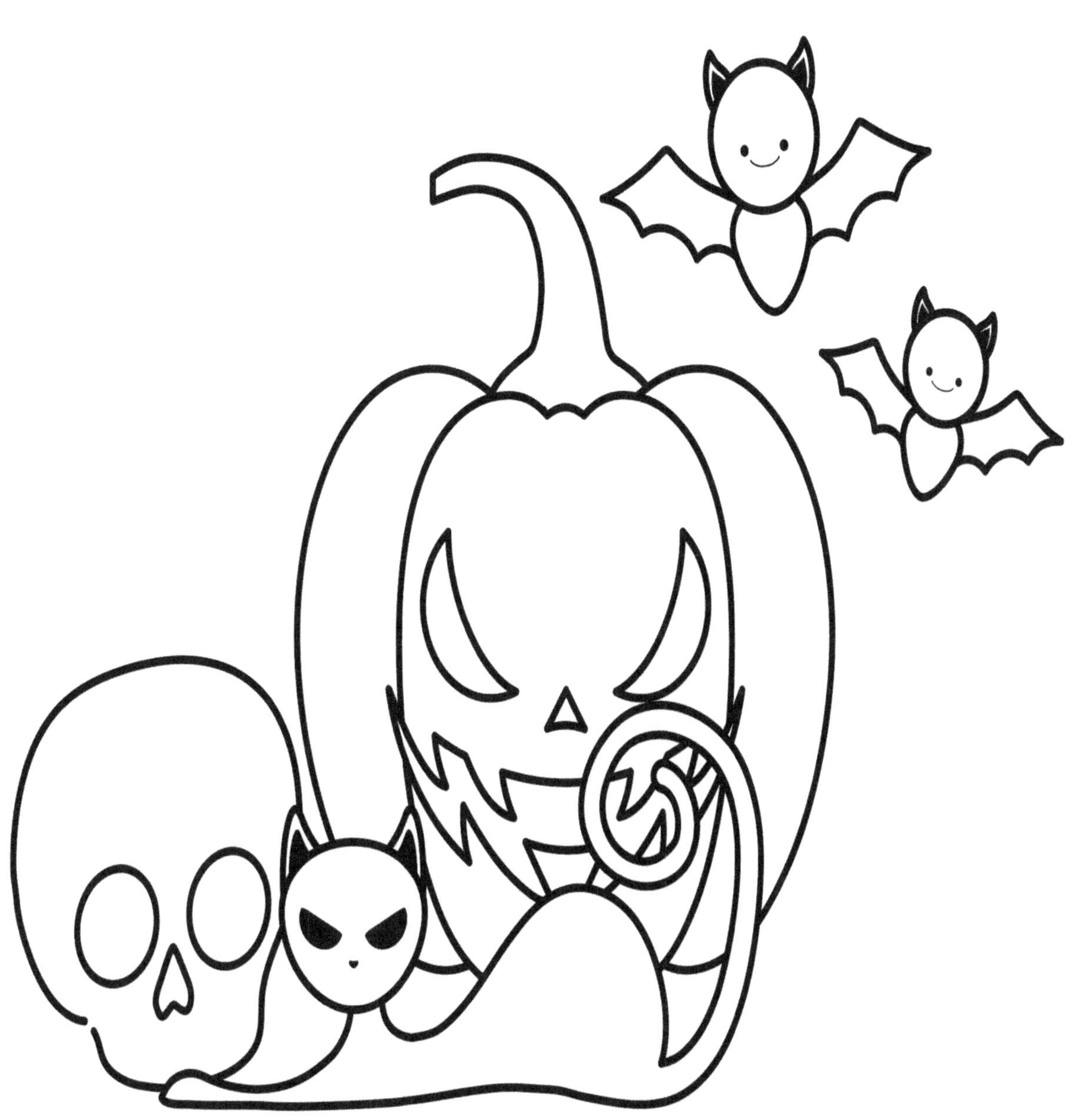

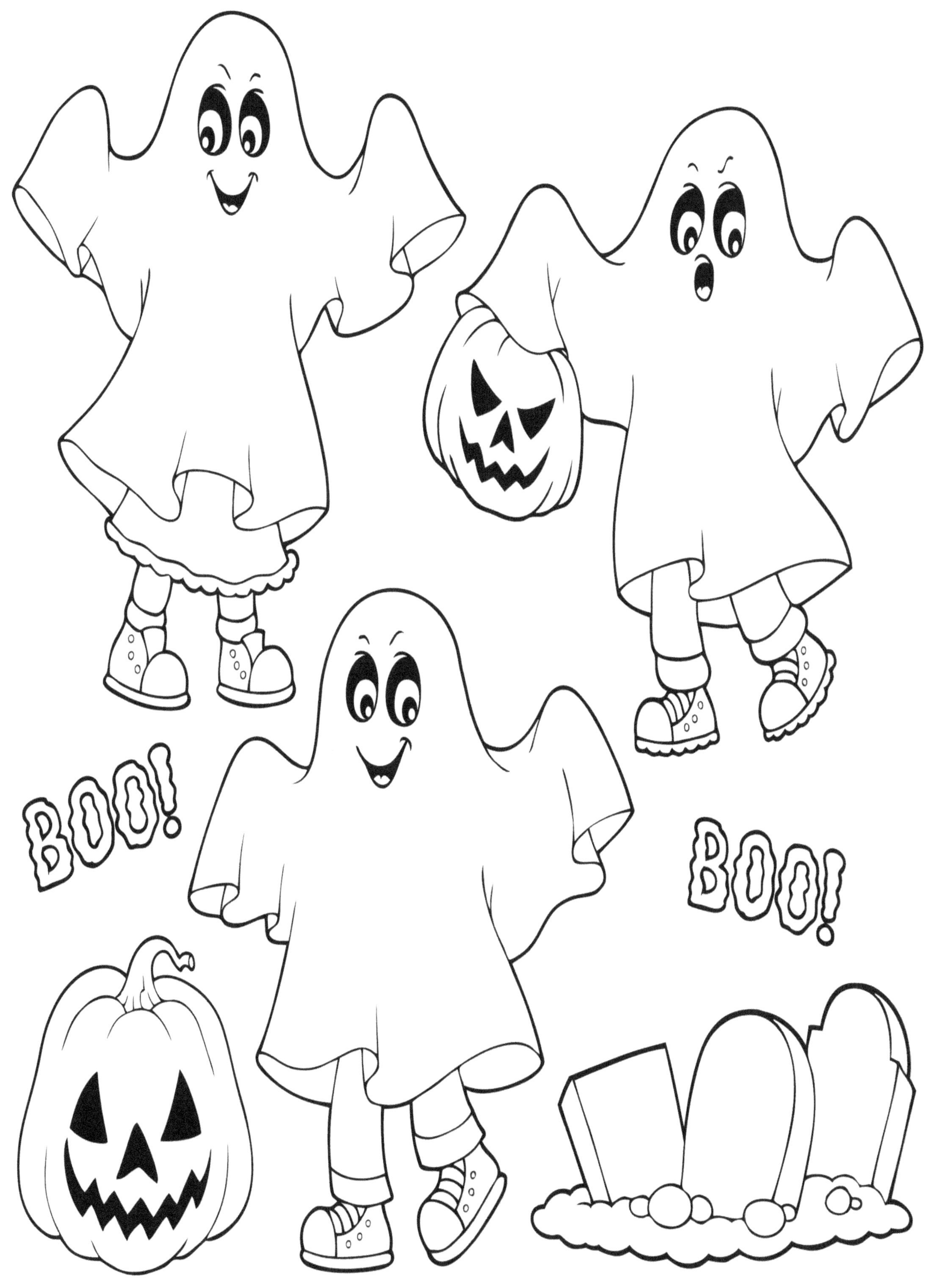

BOO!
BOO!

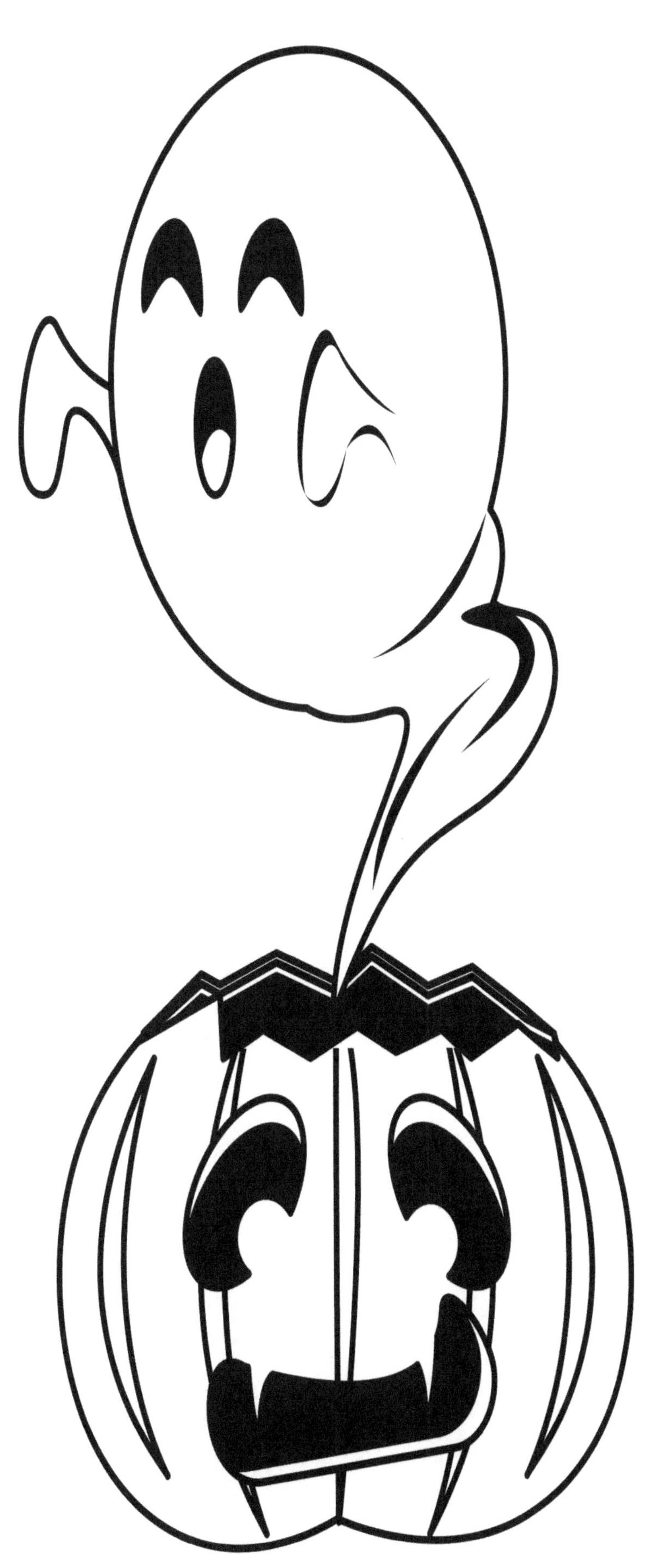

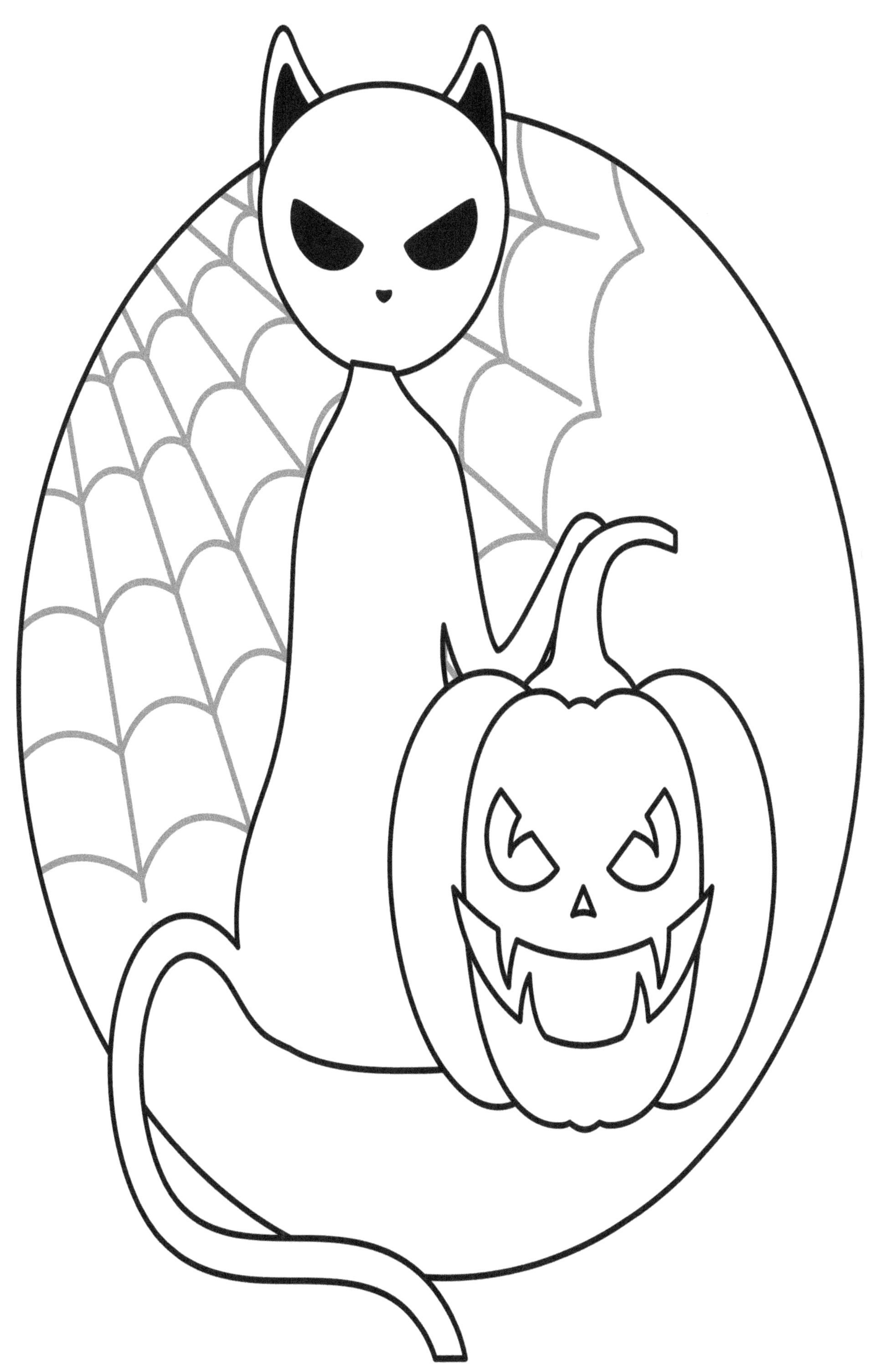

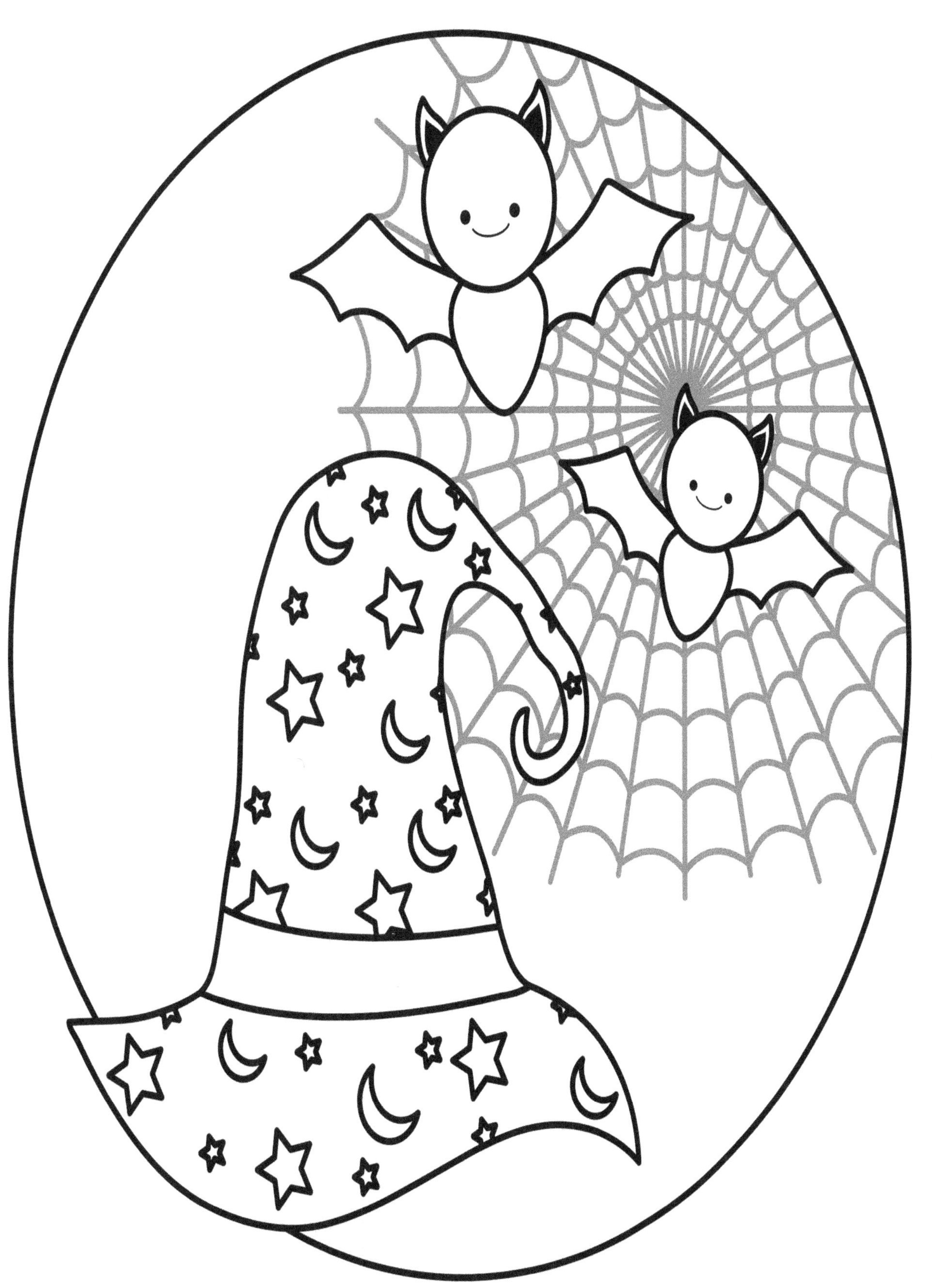

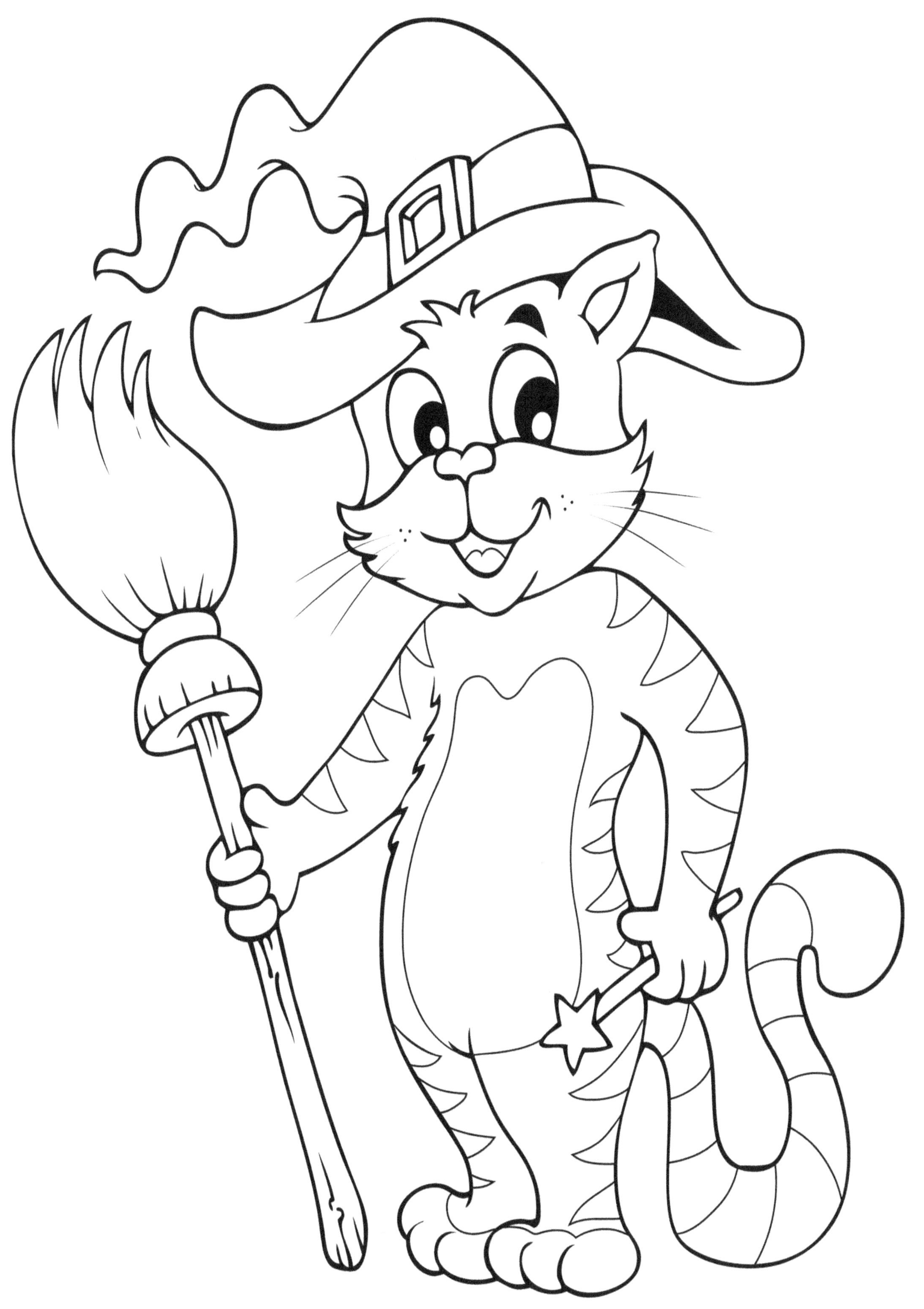

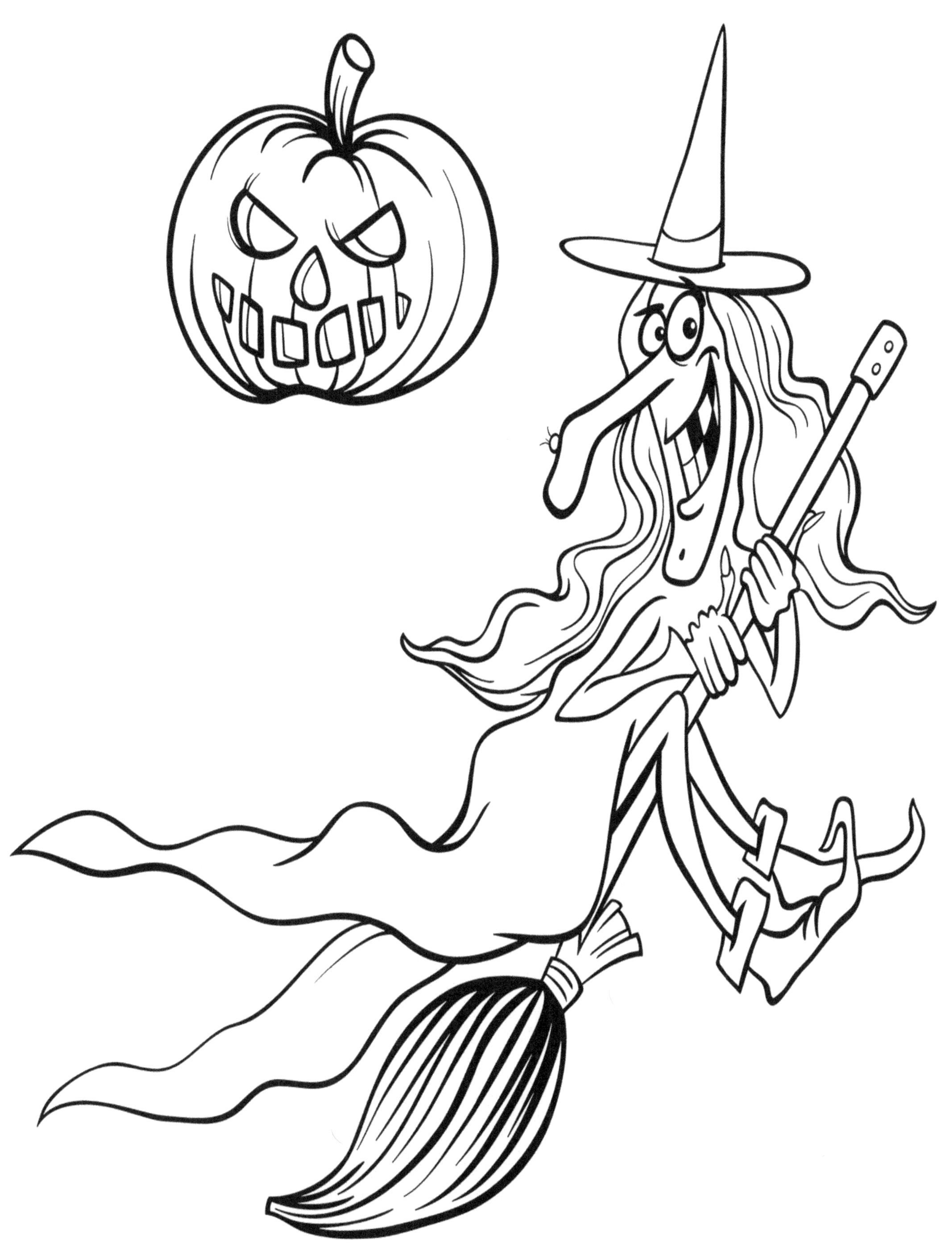

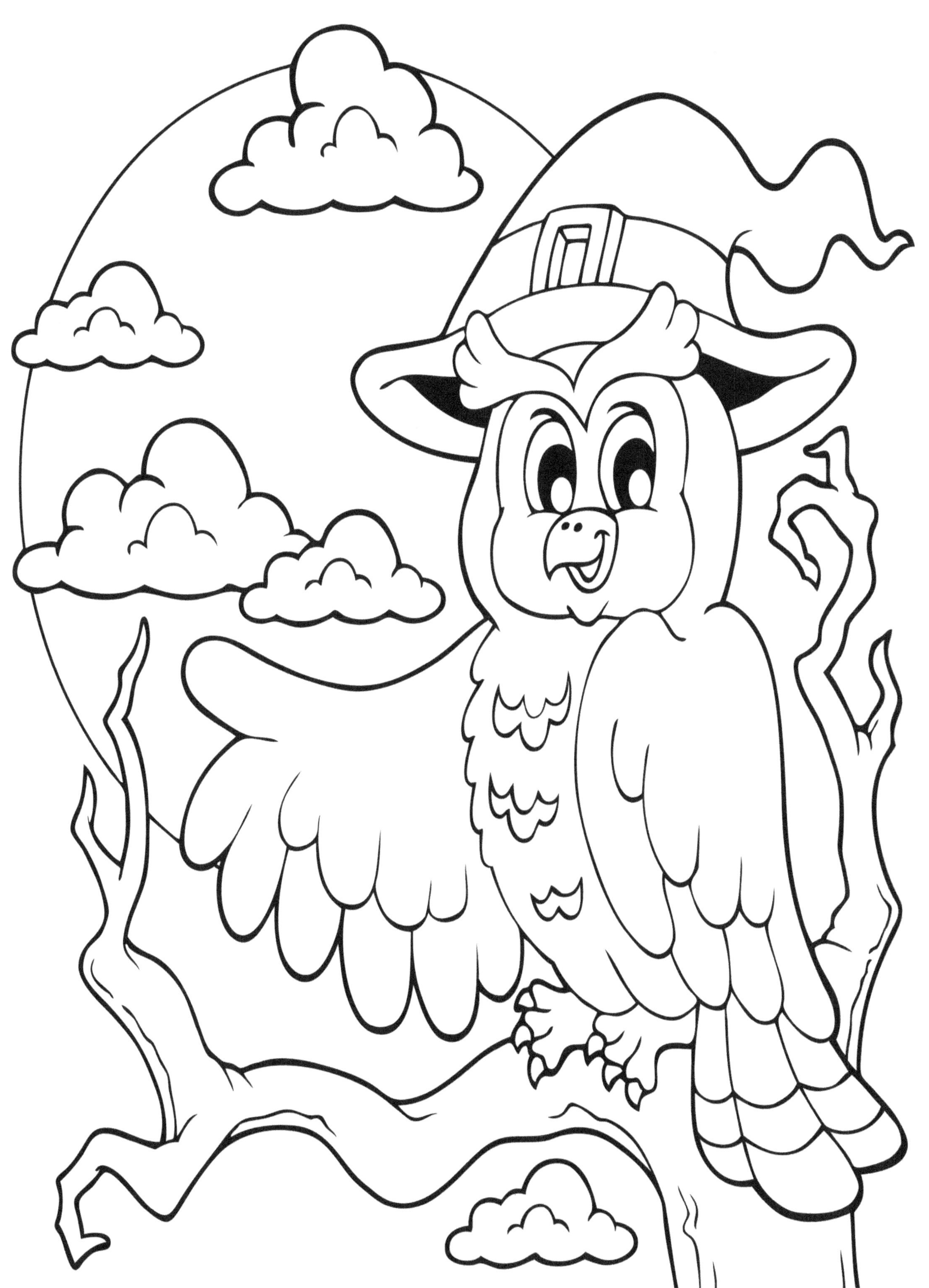

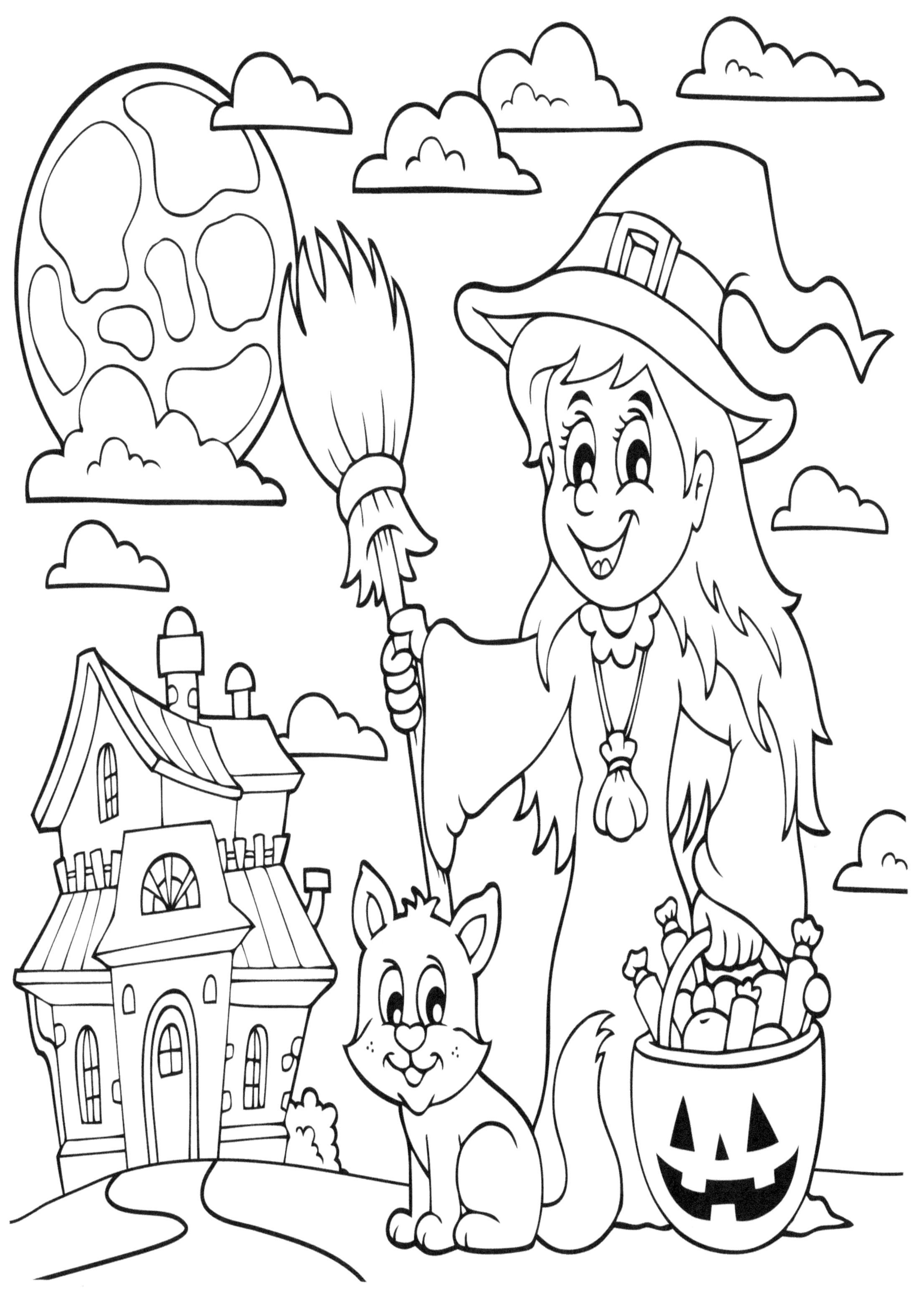

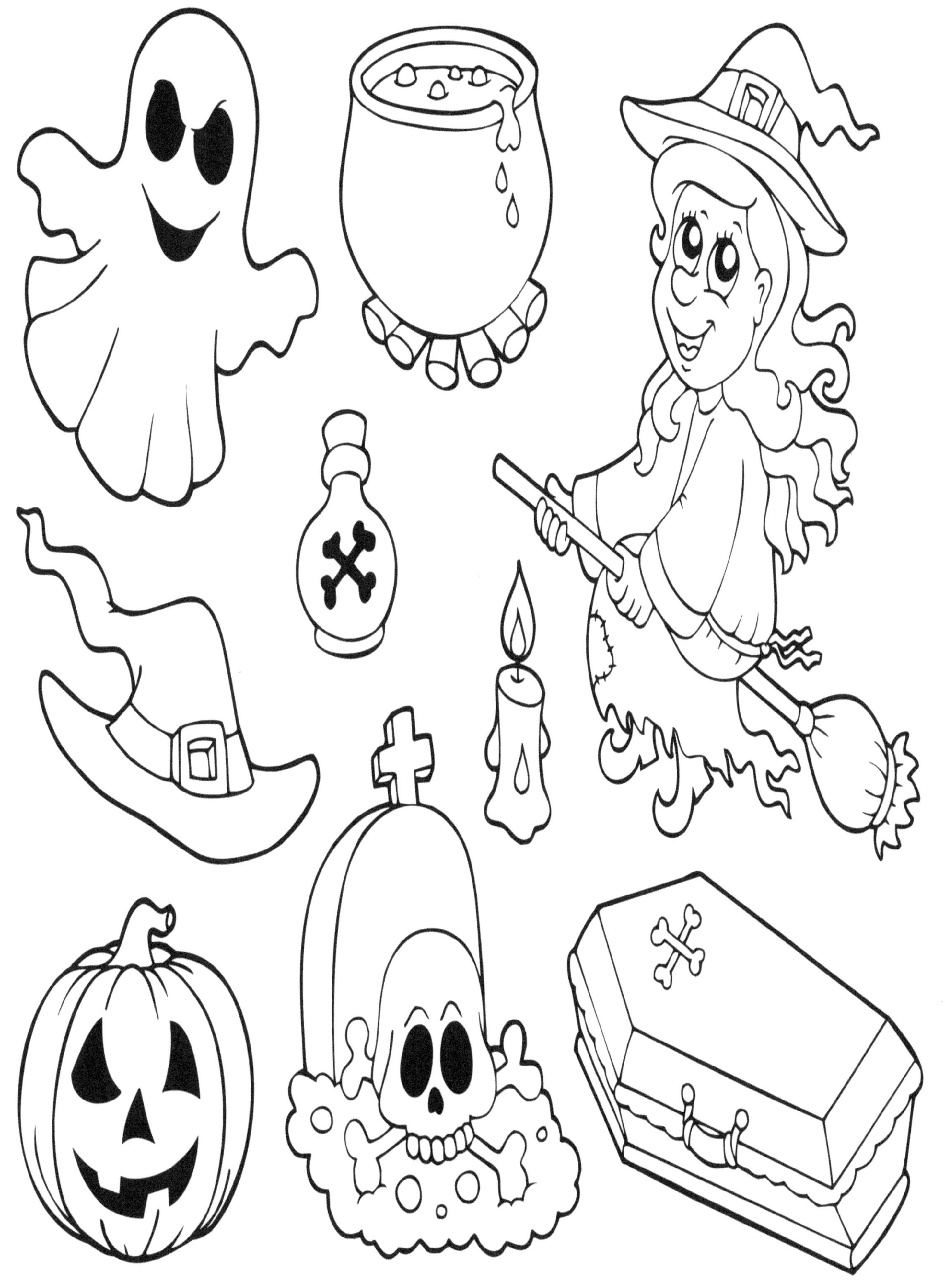

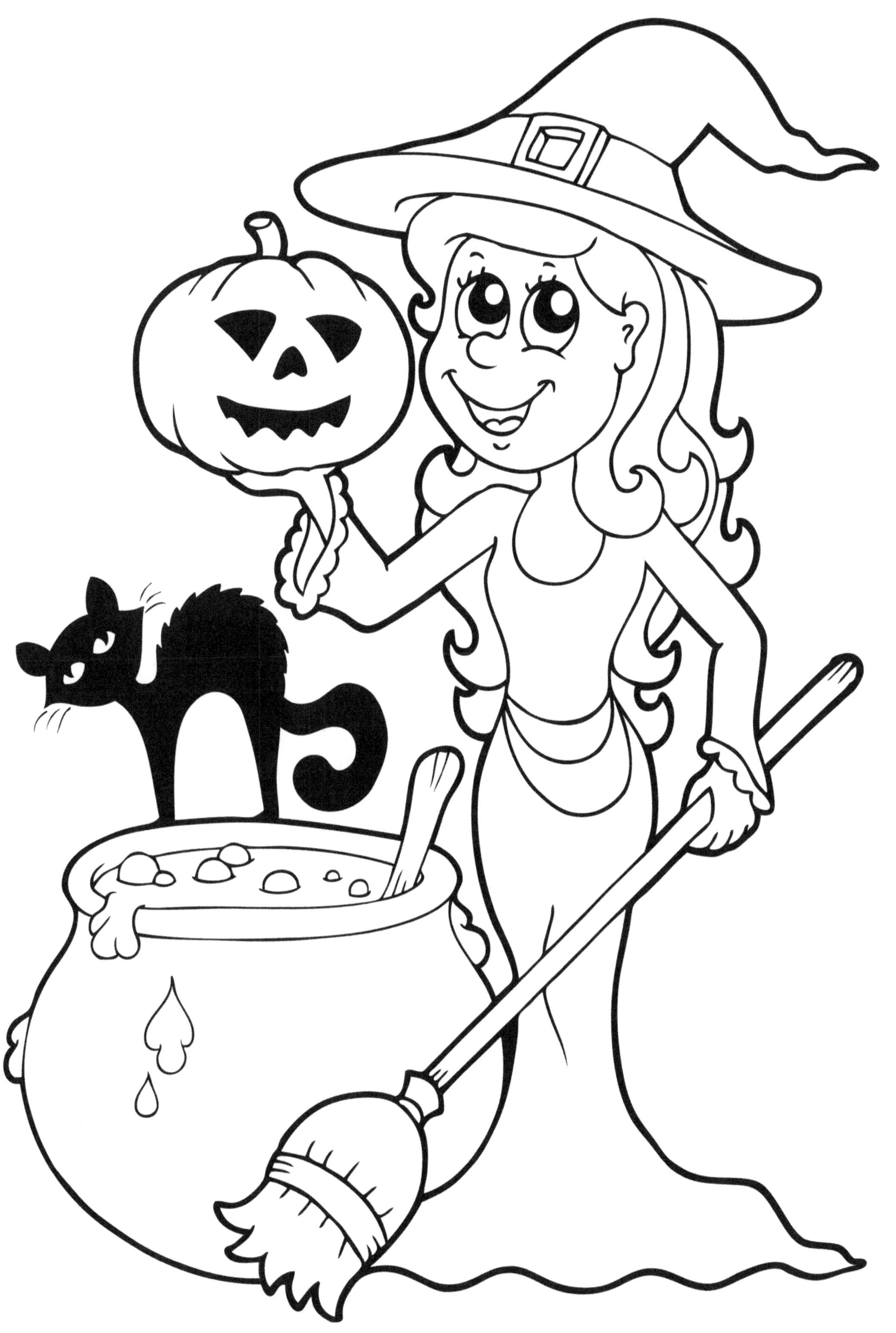

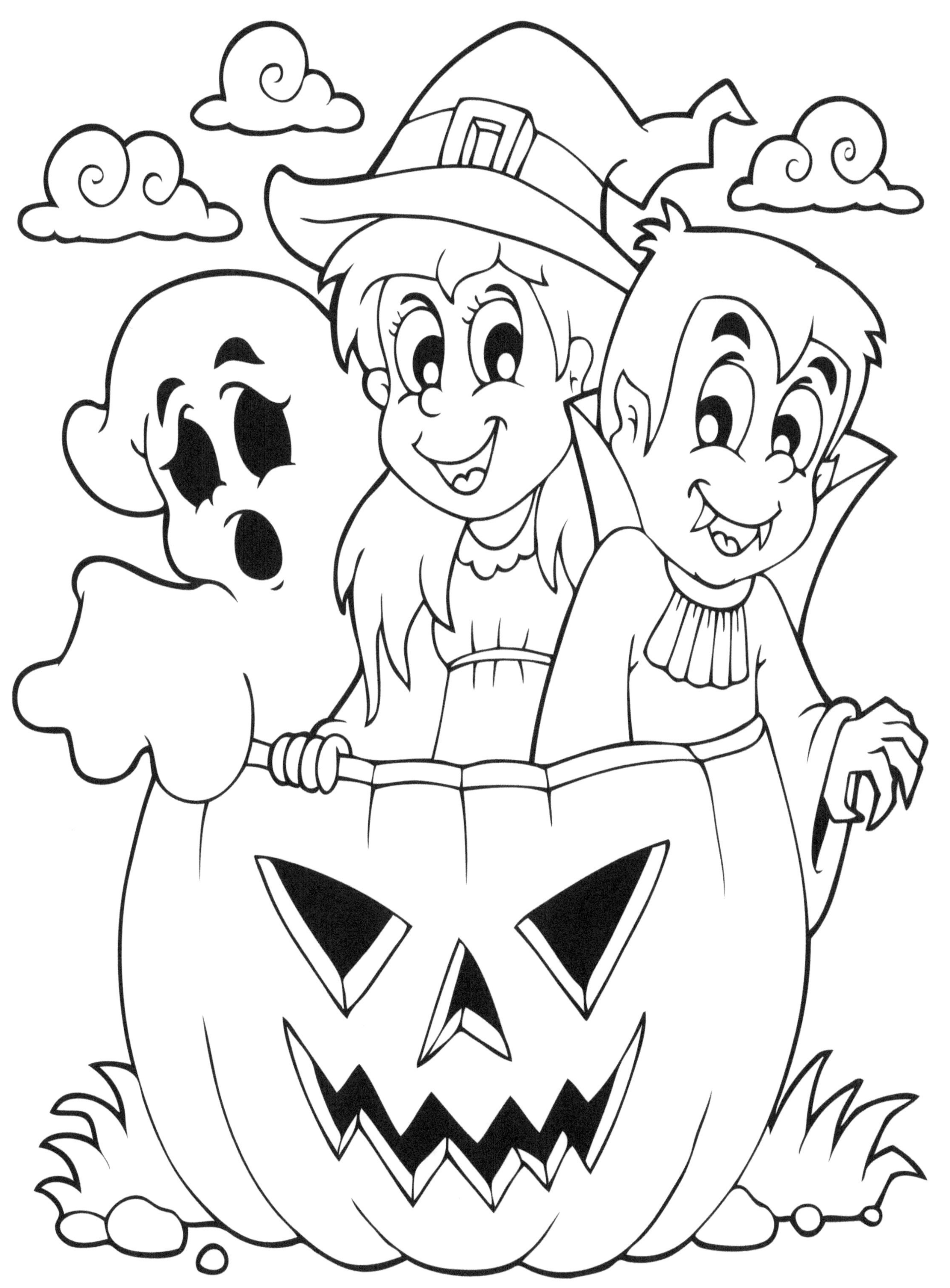

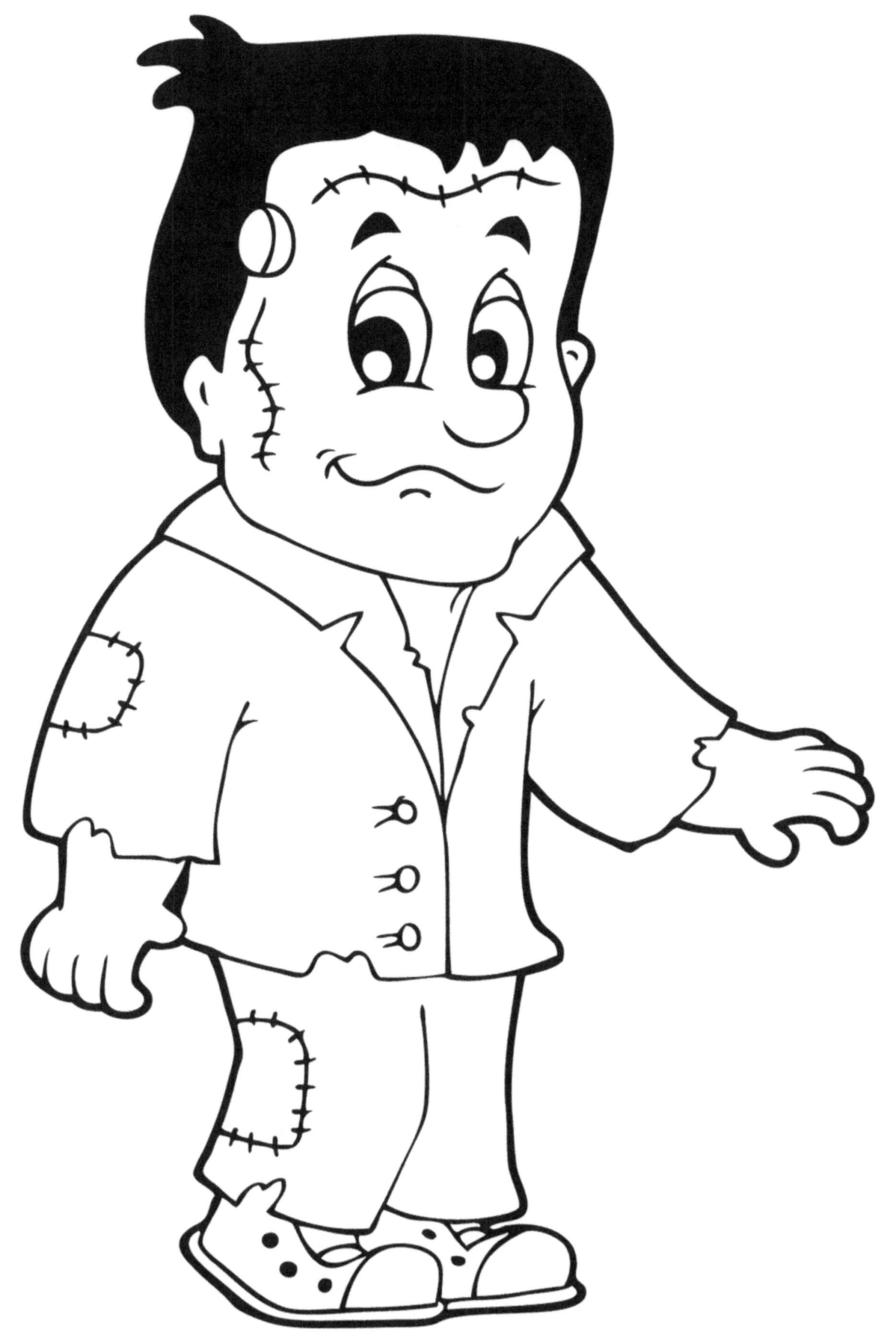

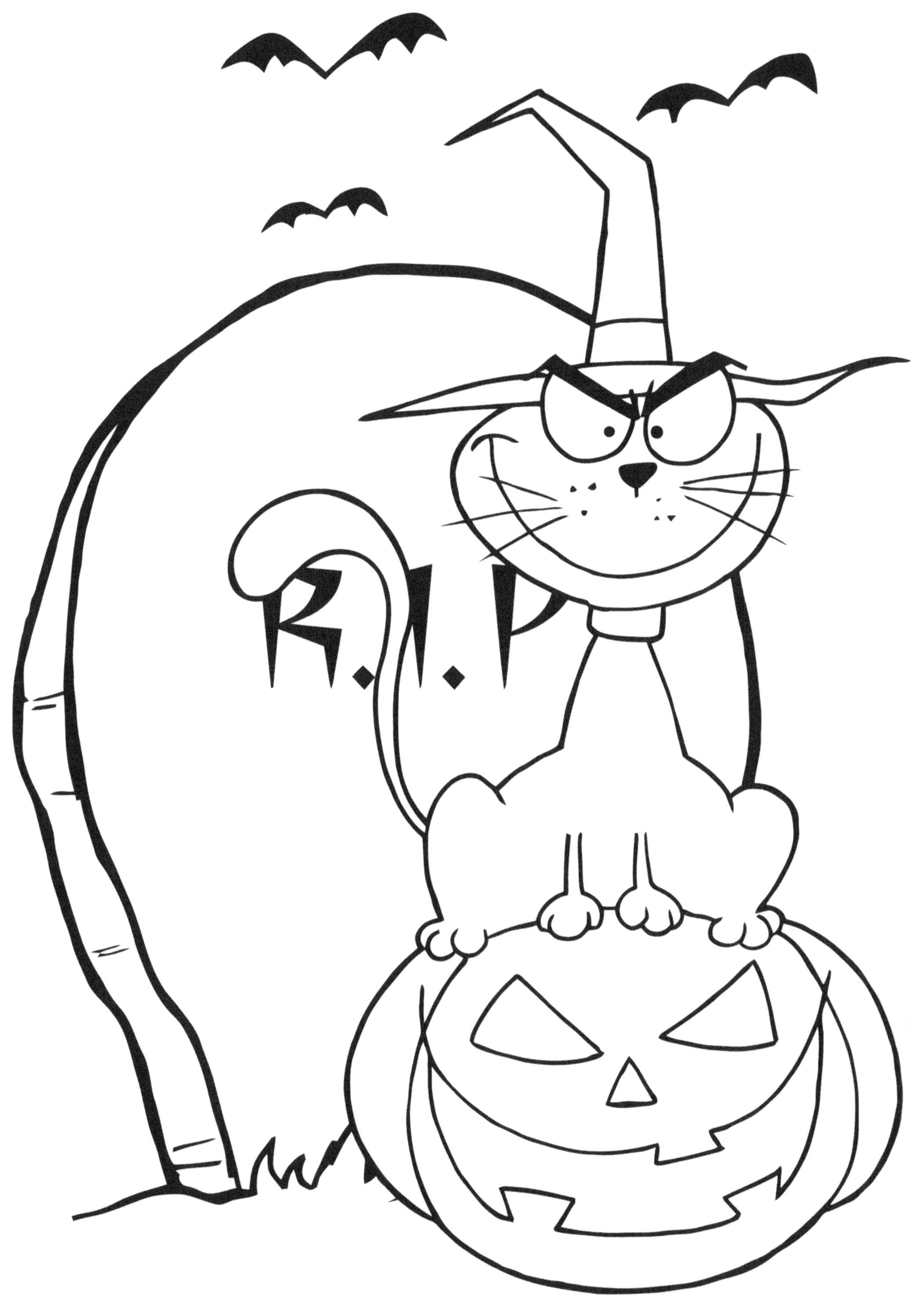
R.I.P.

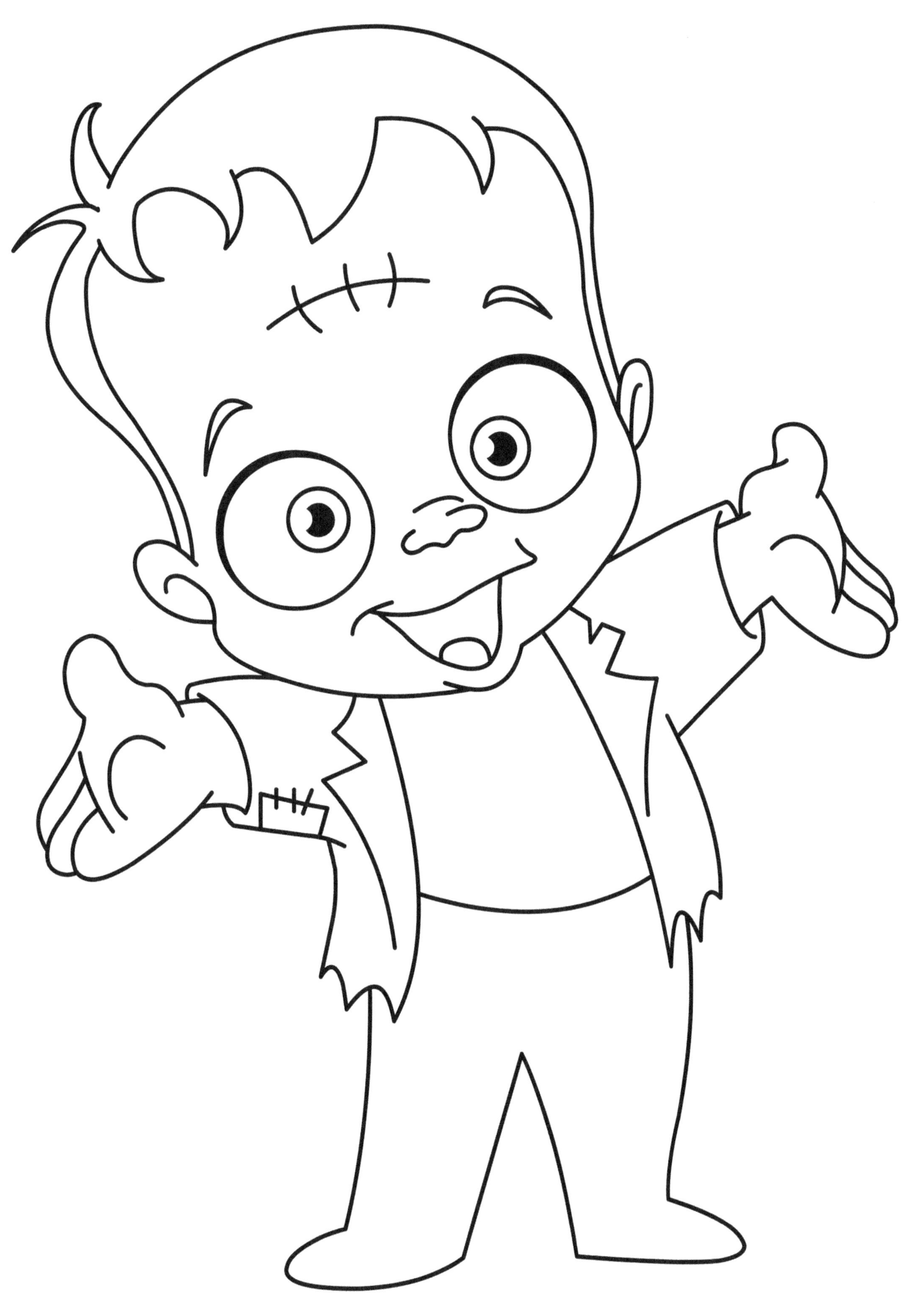

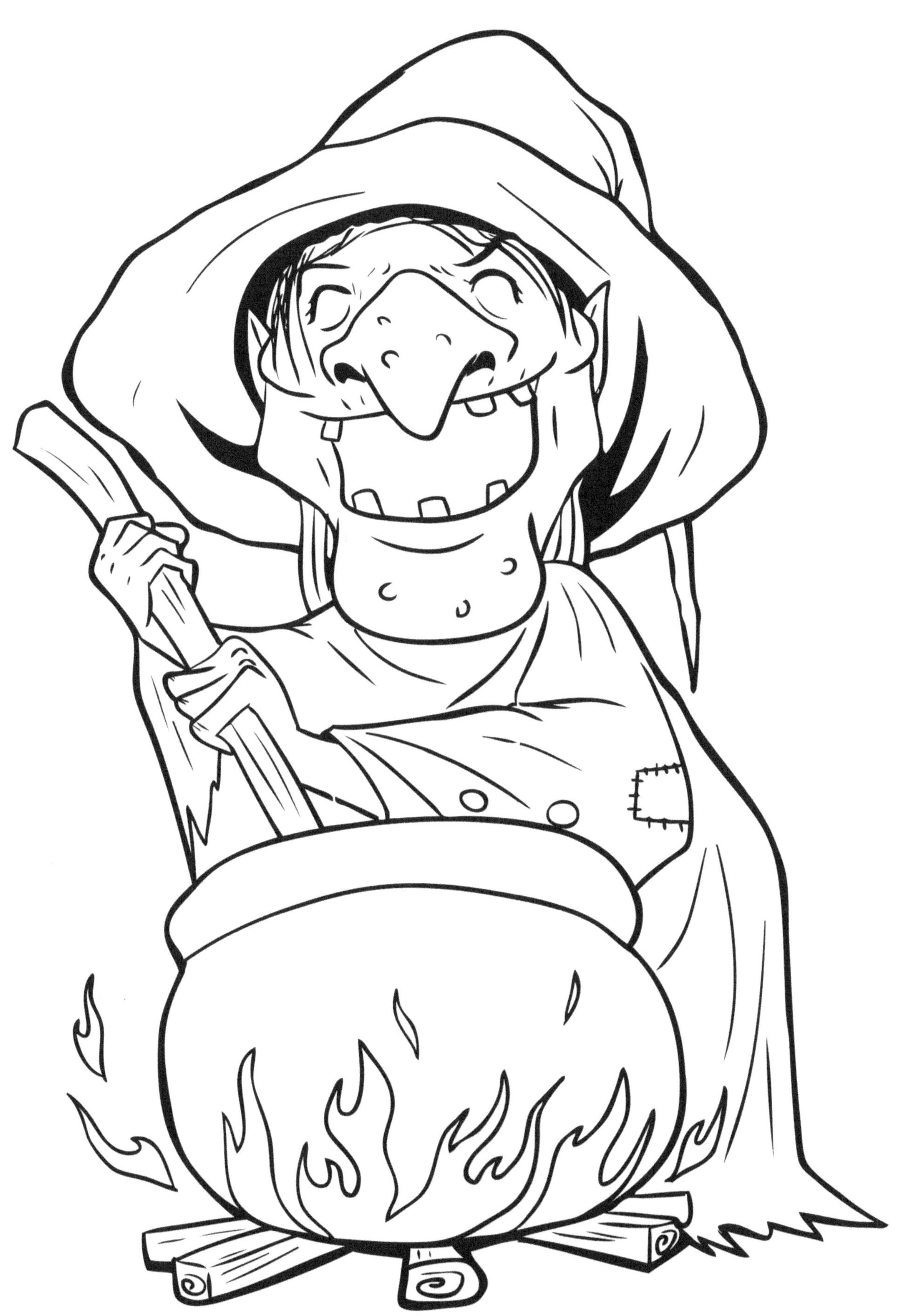

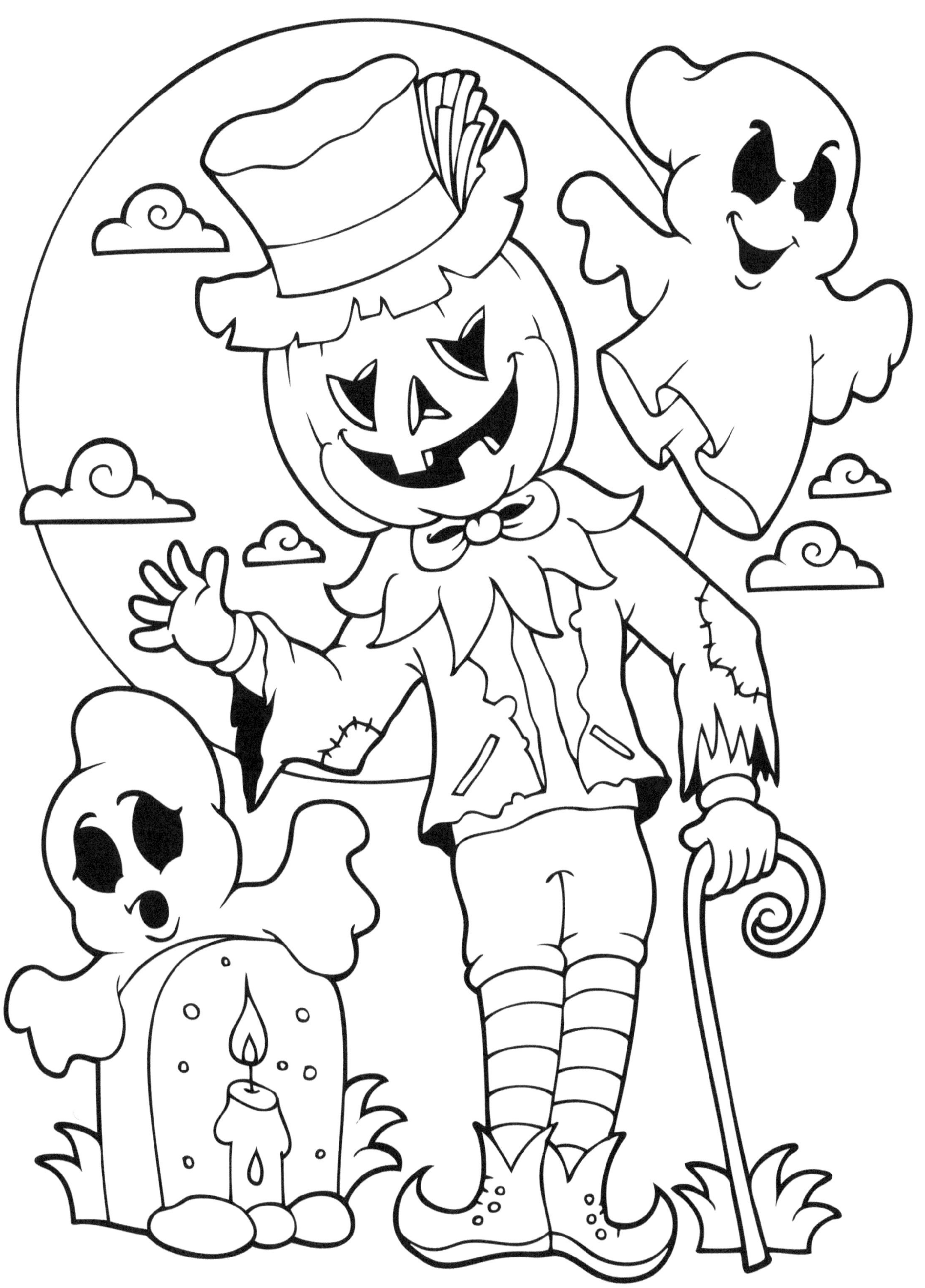

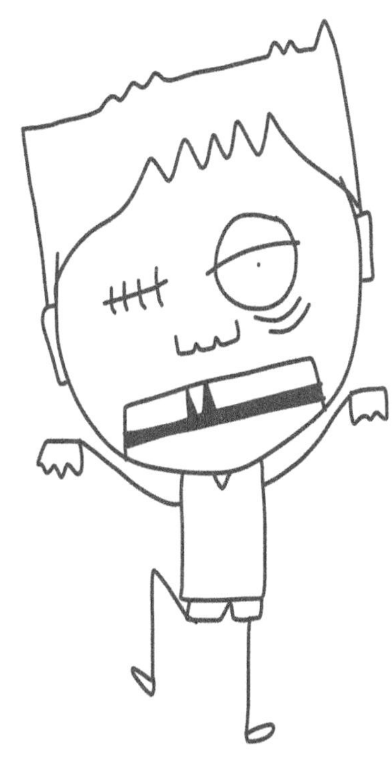
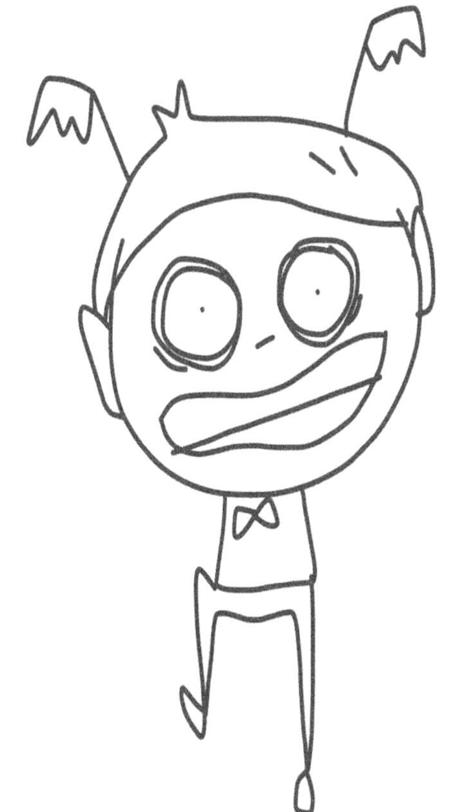
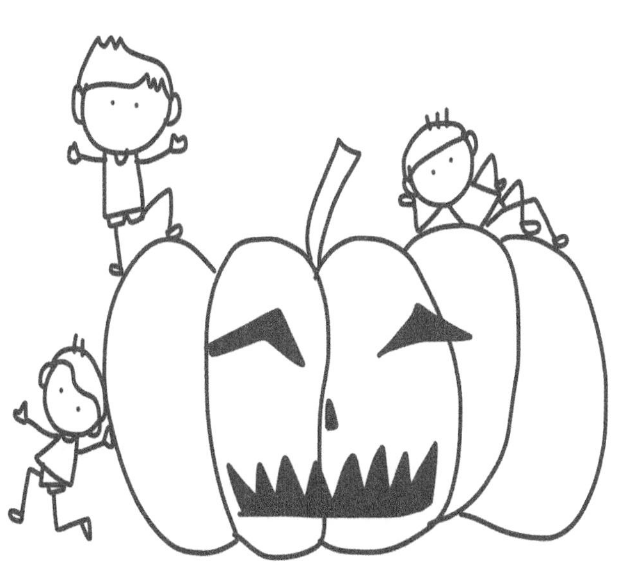
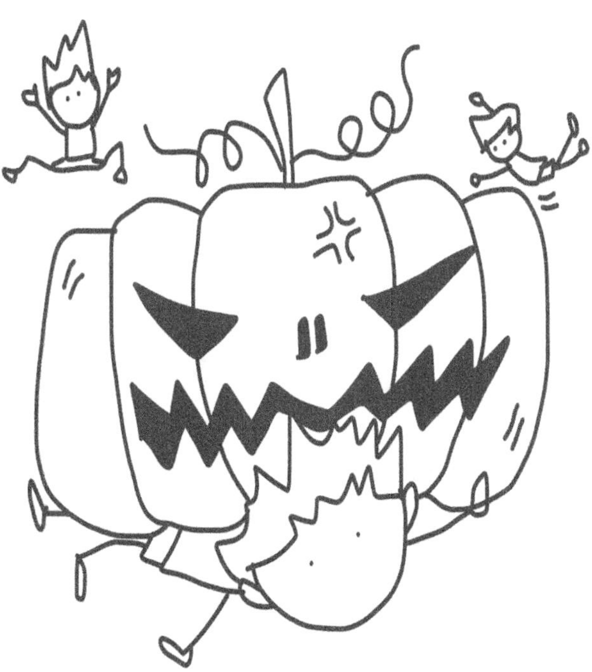

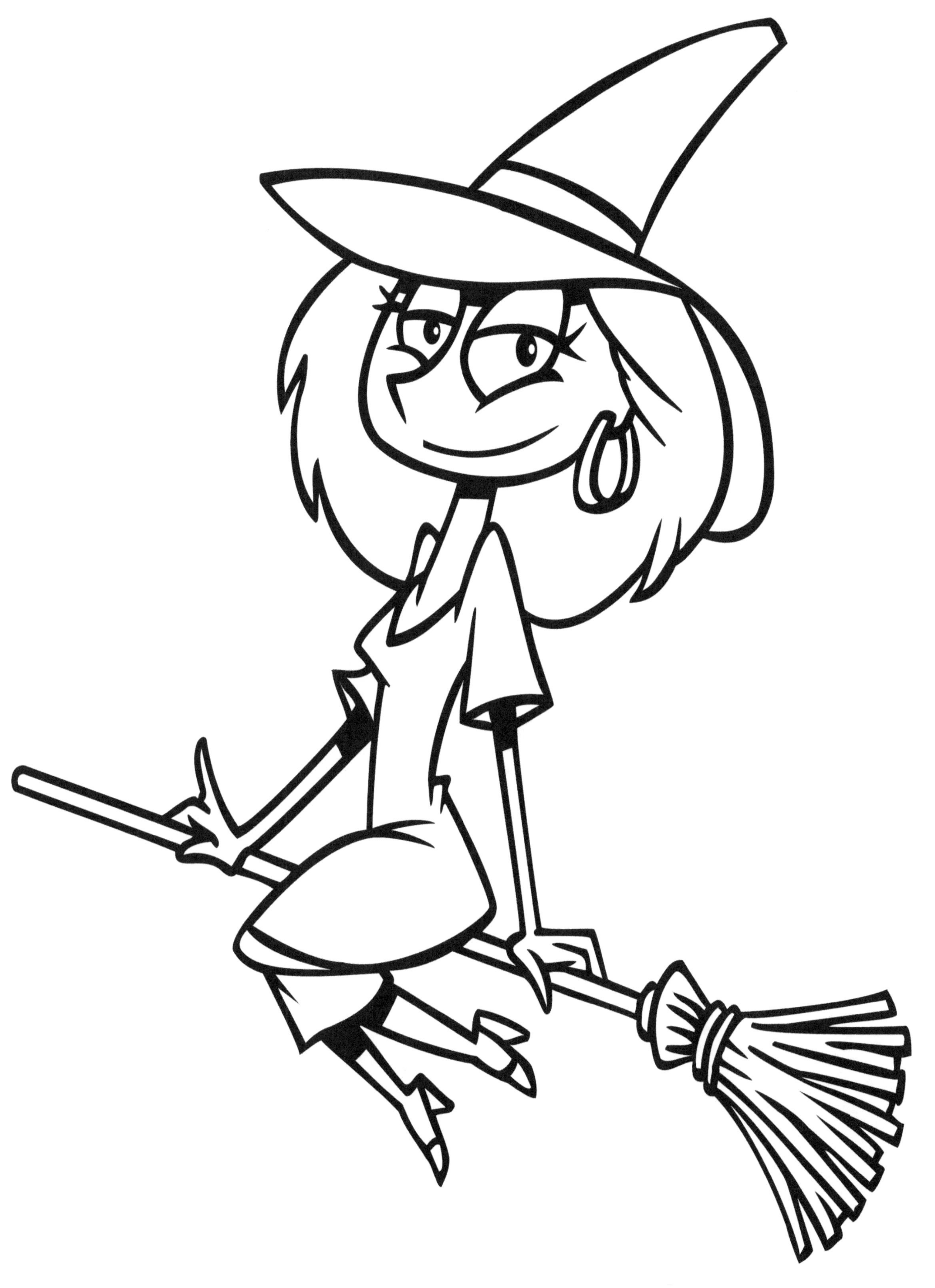

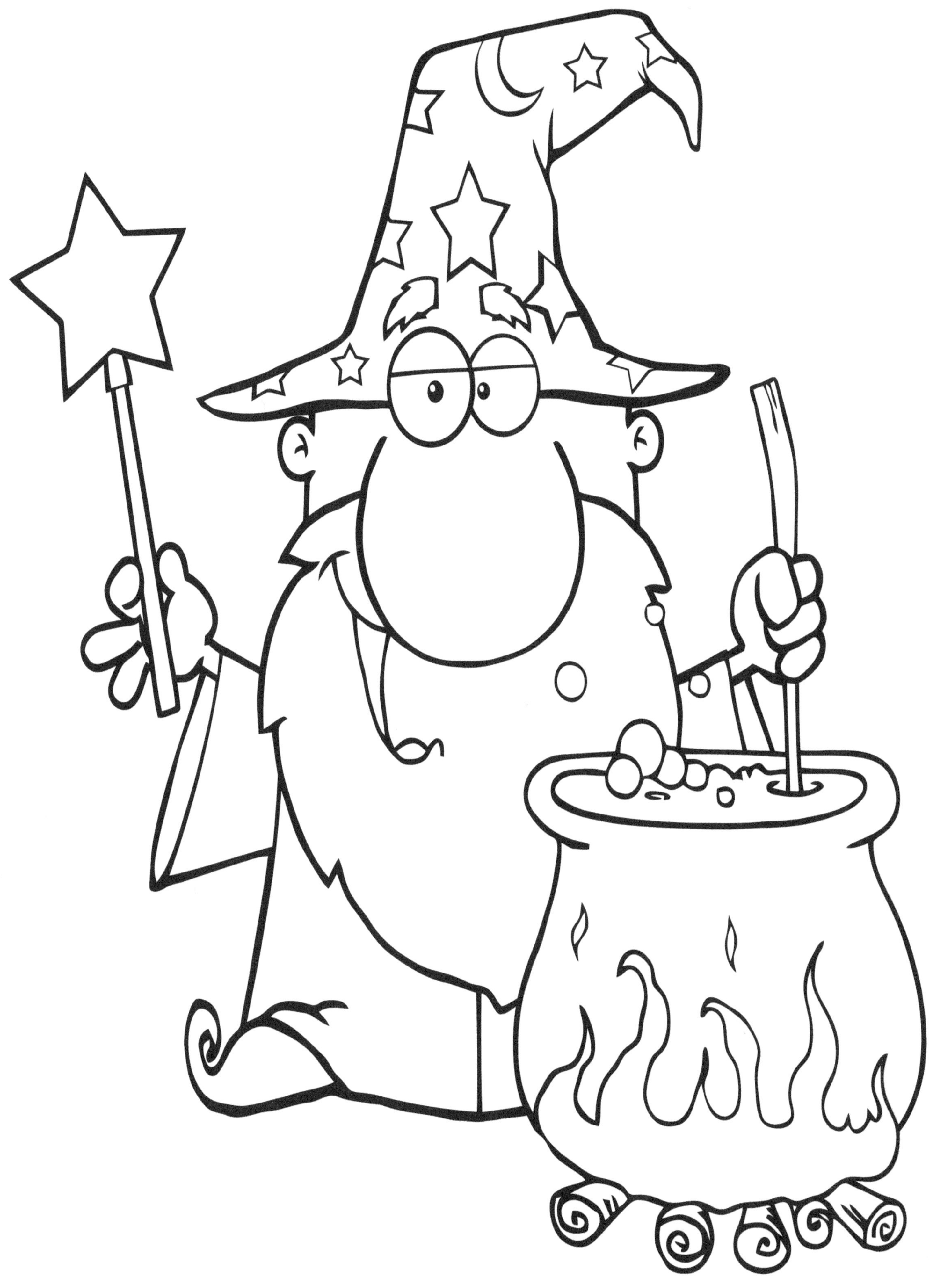

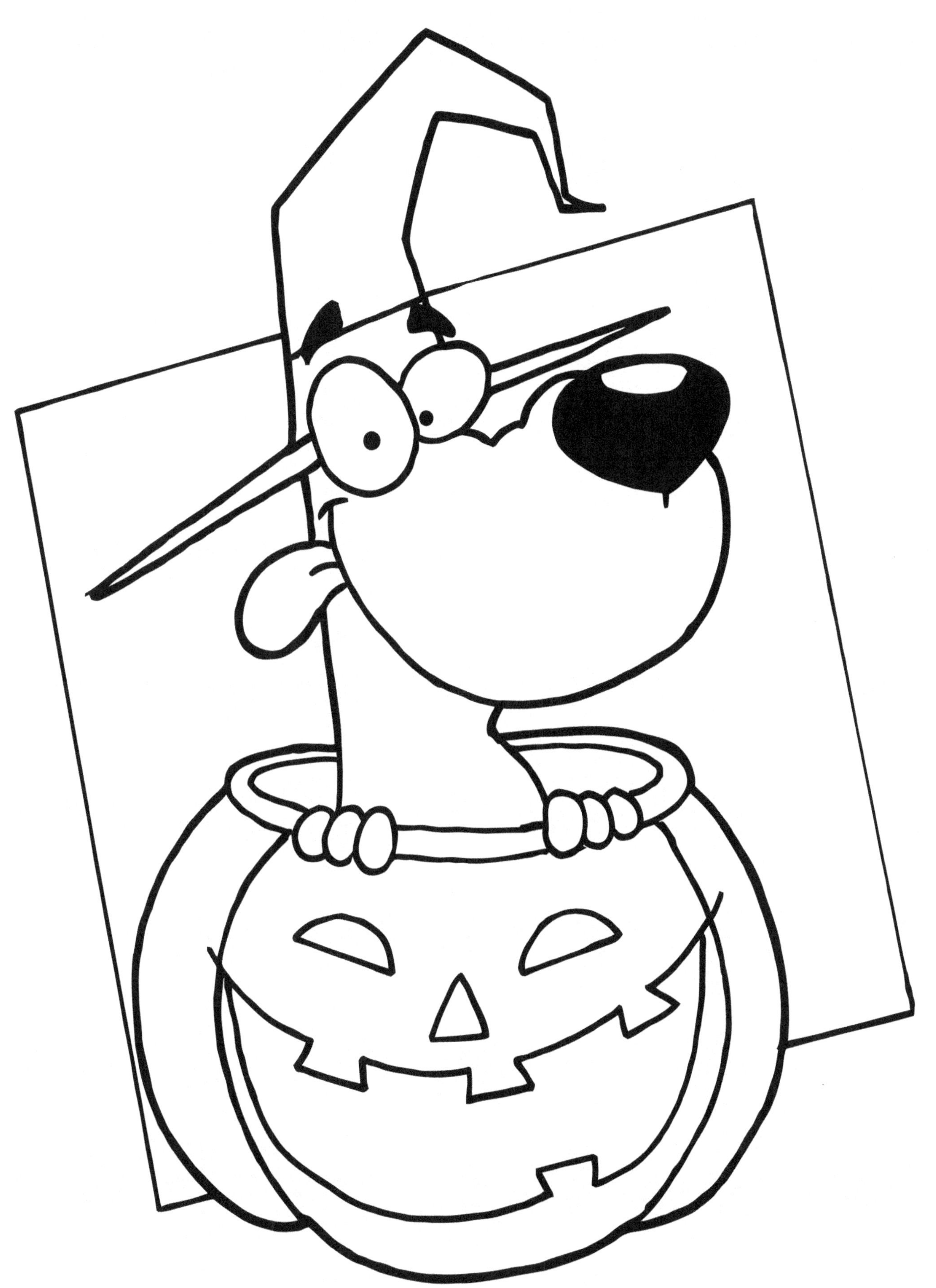

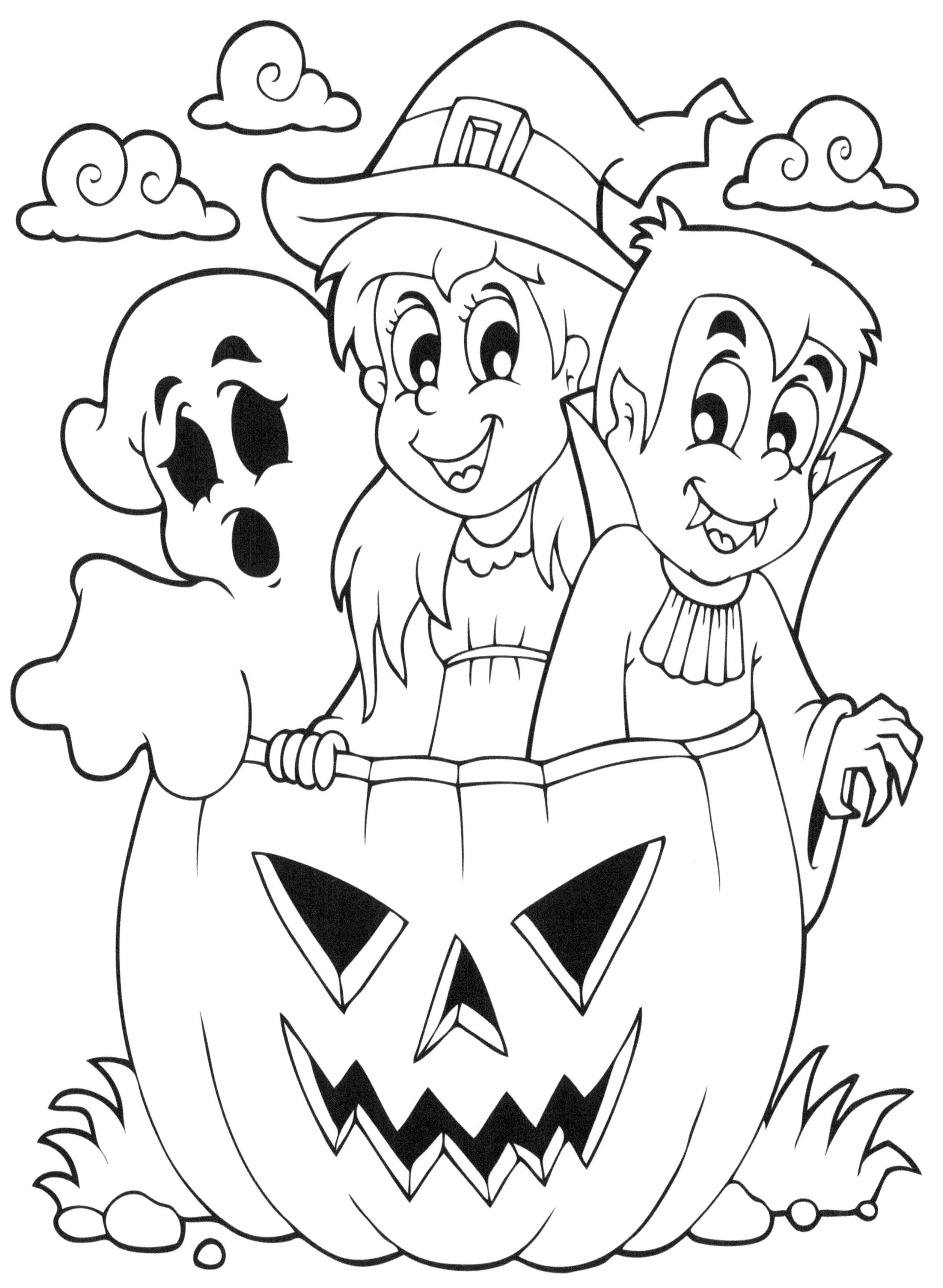

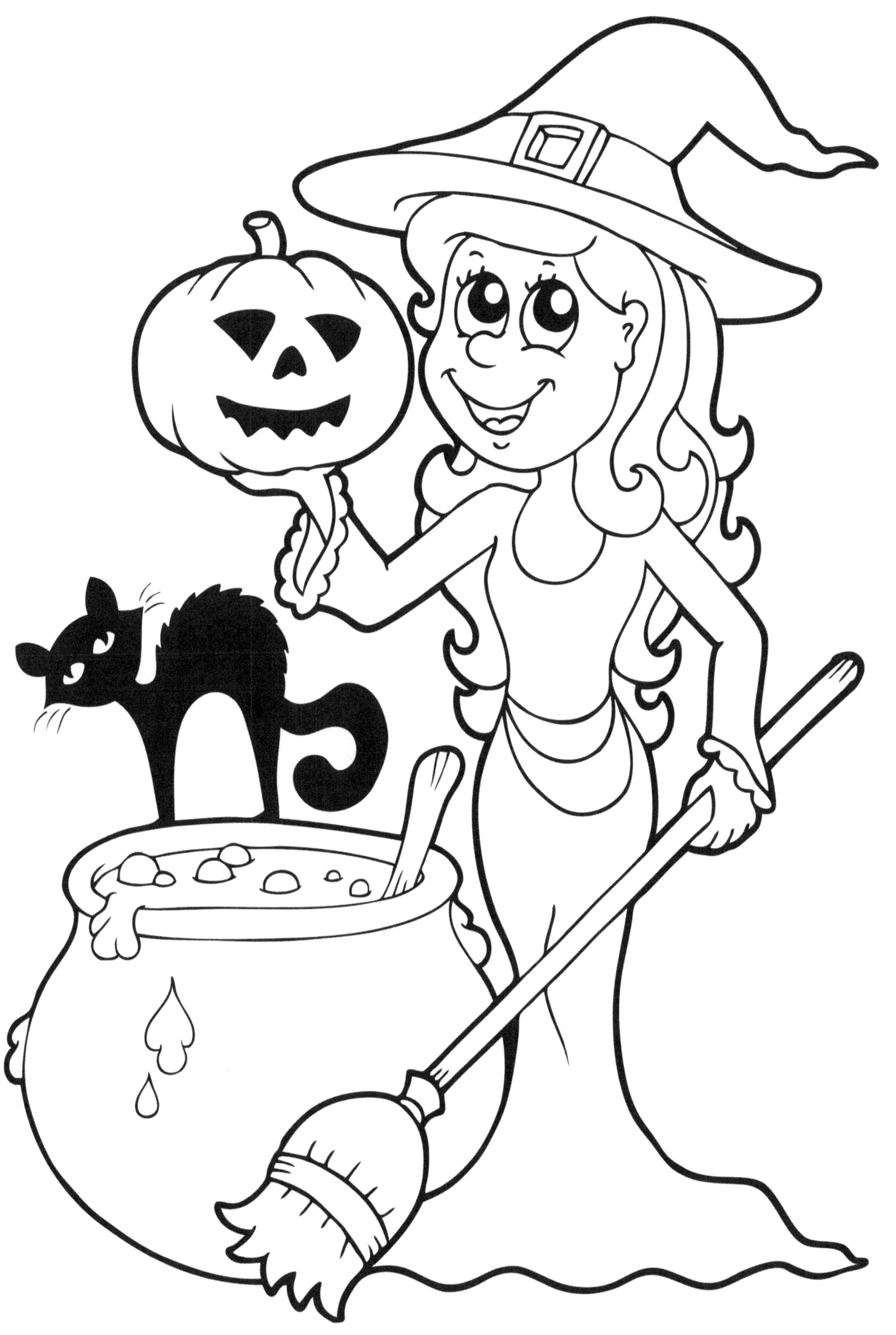

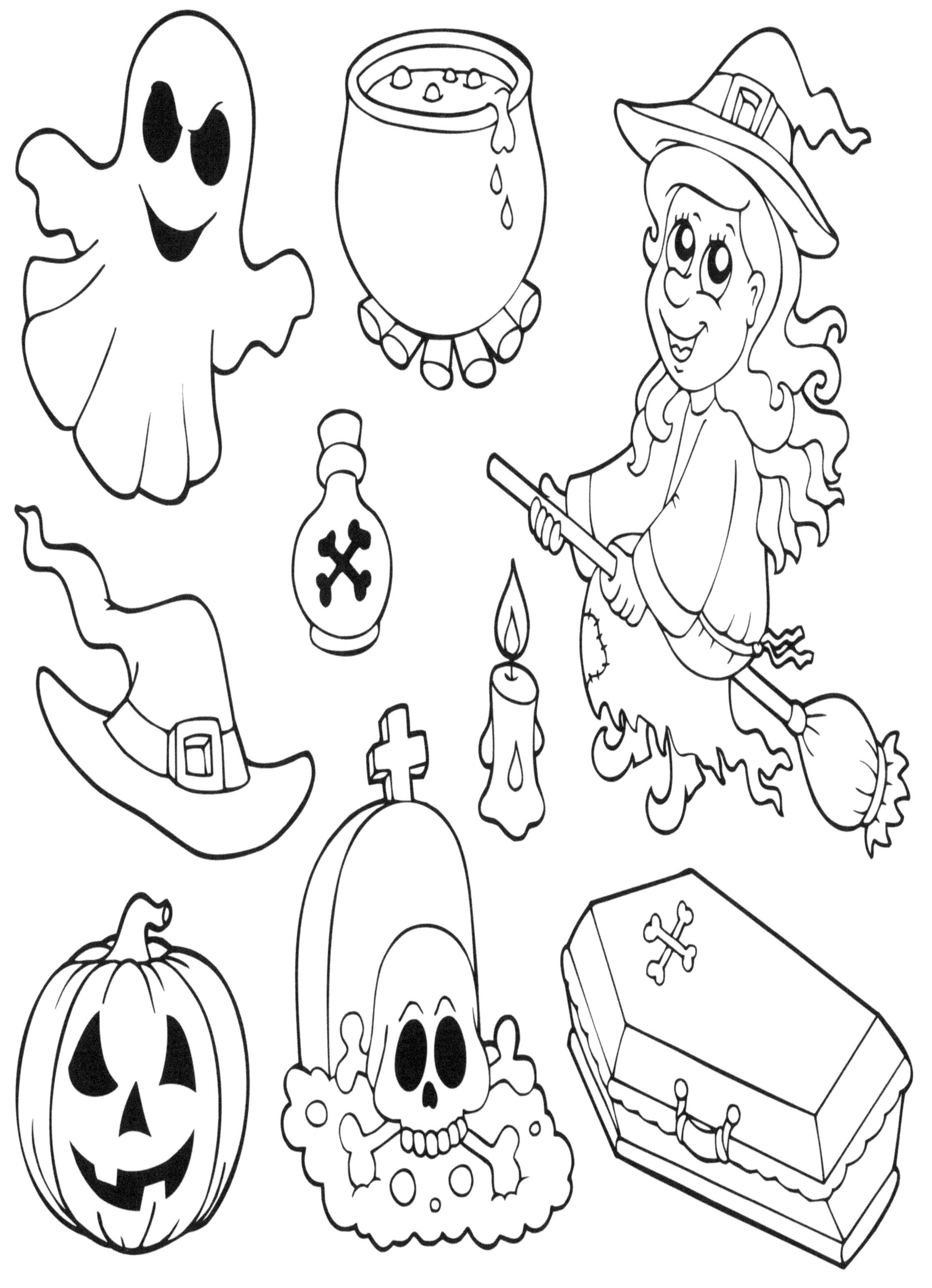

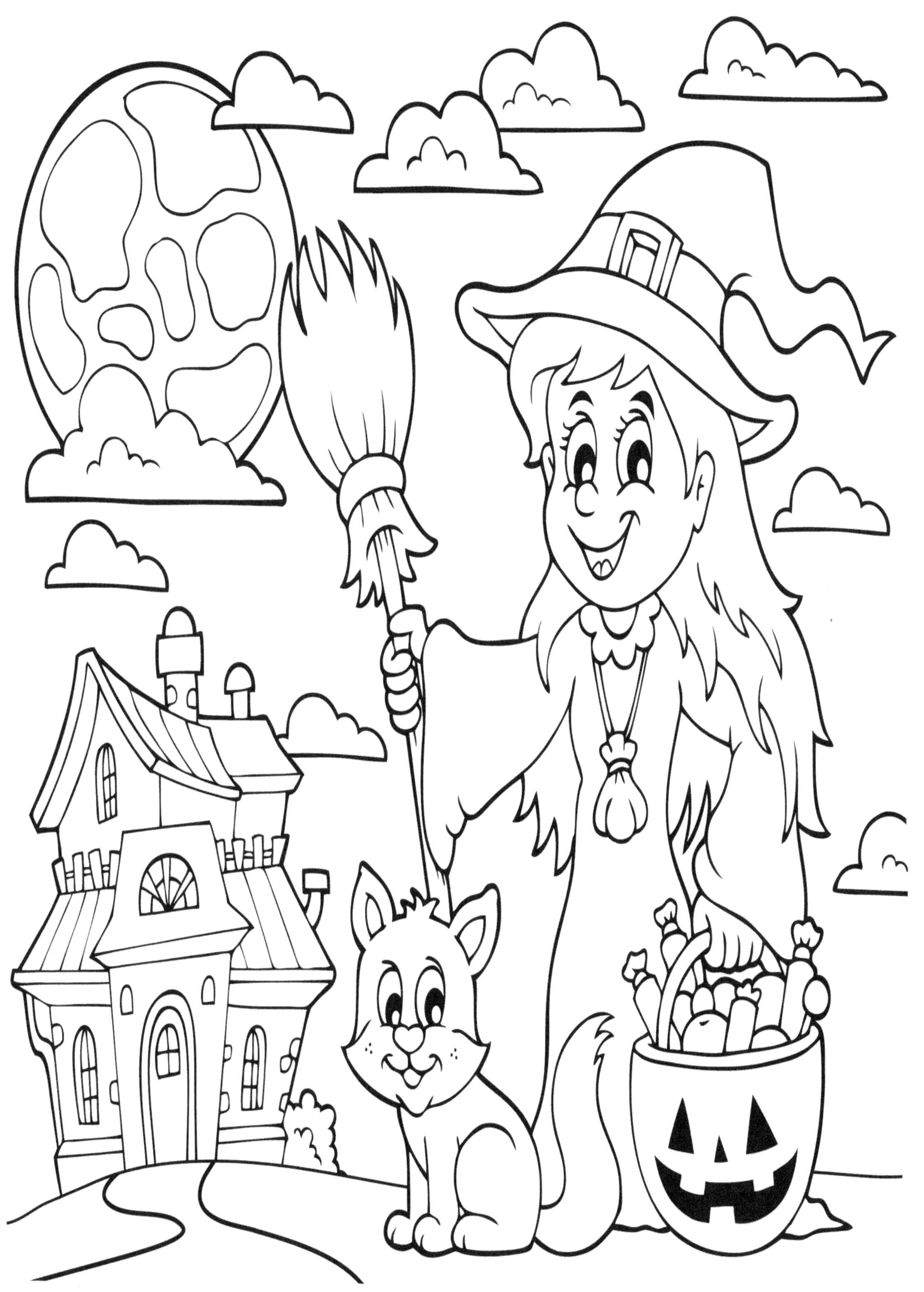

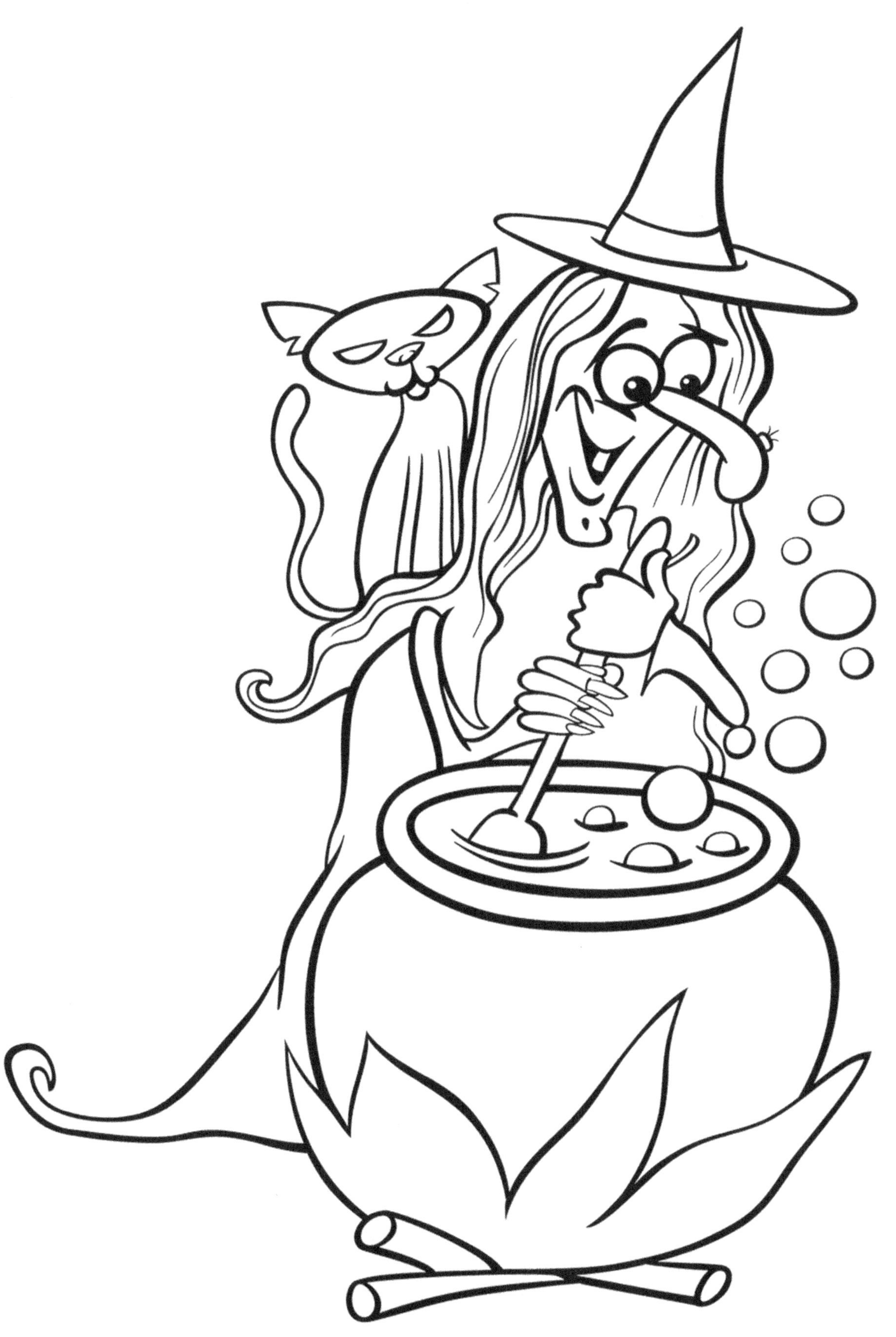

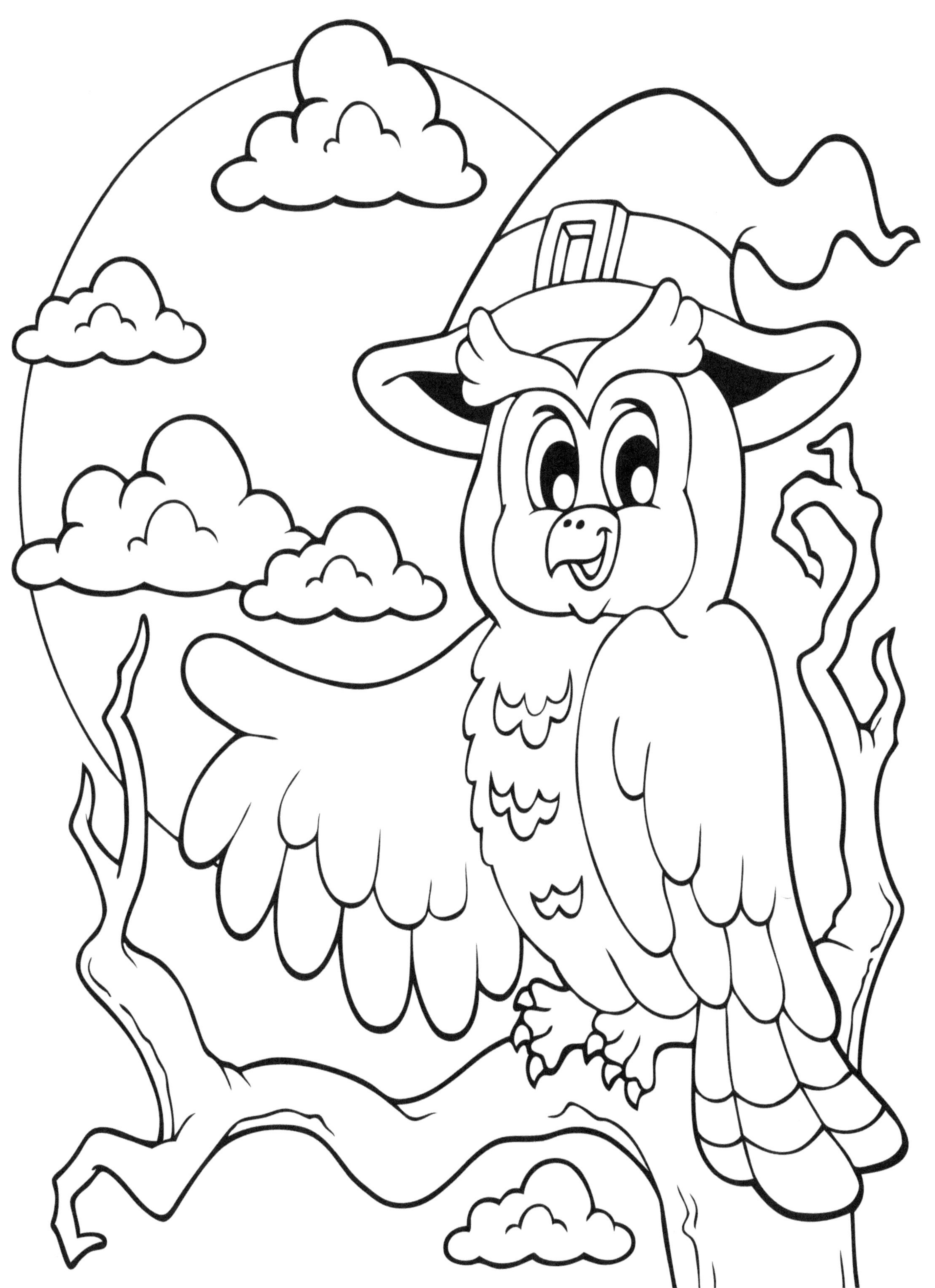

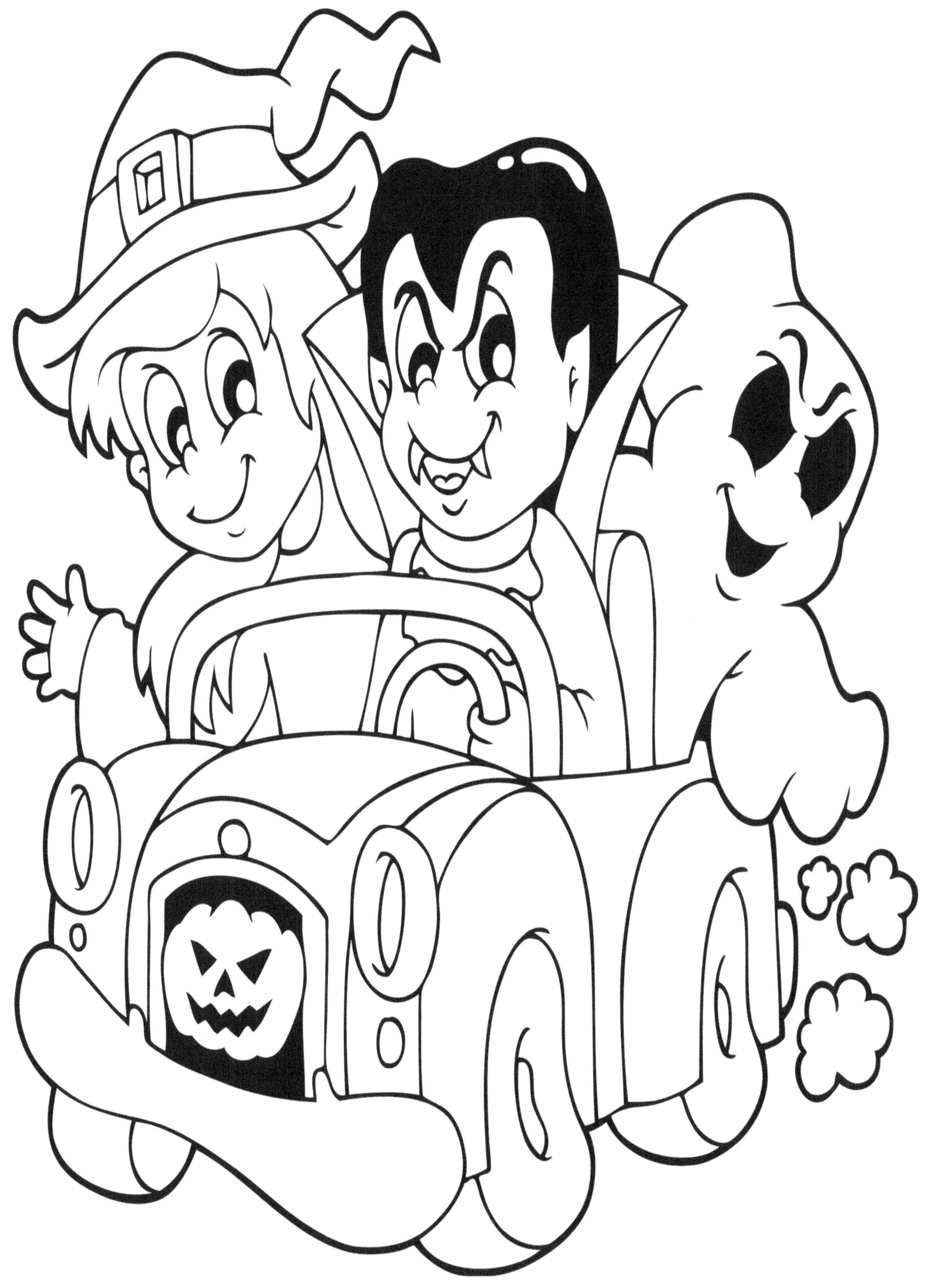

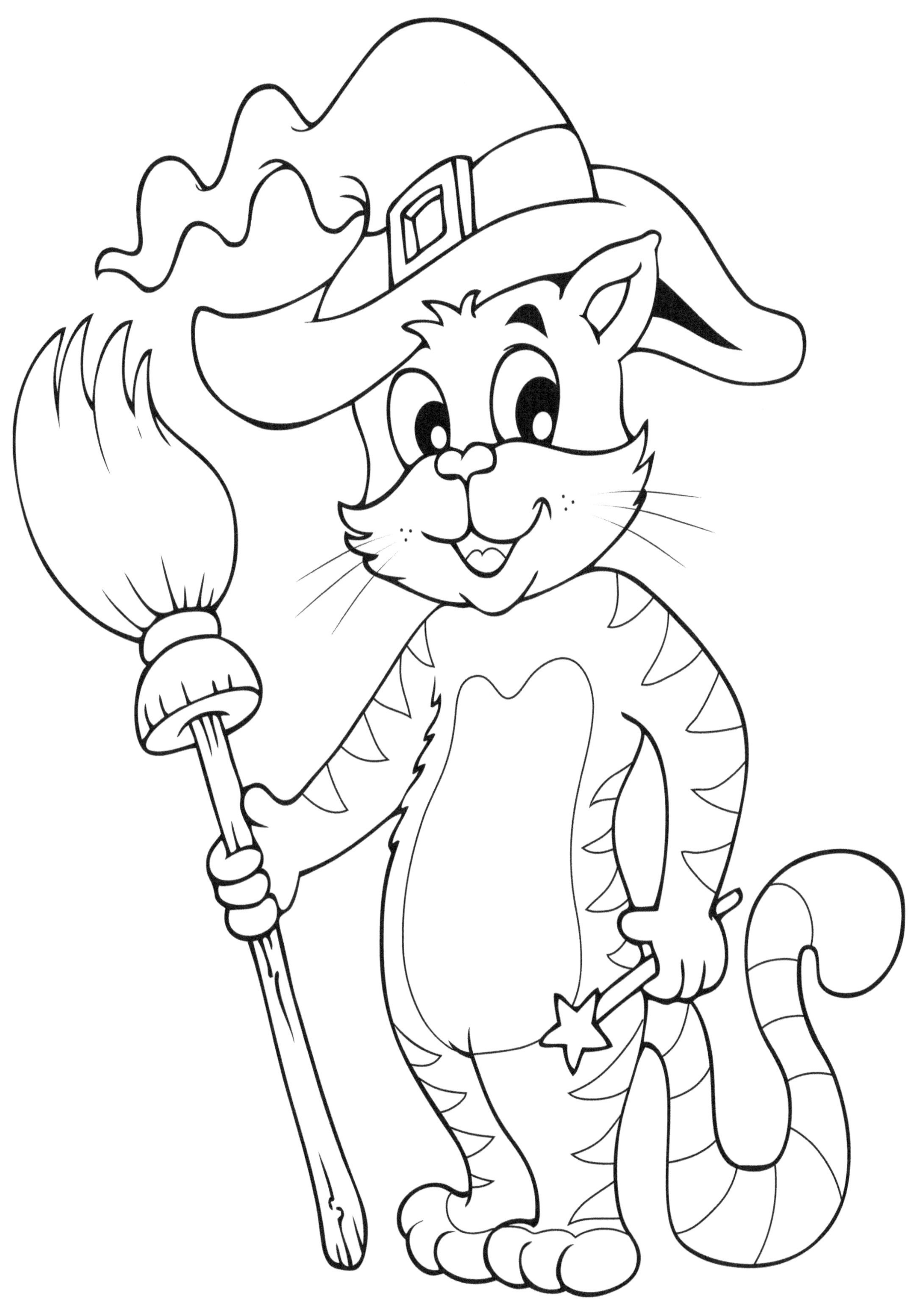

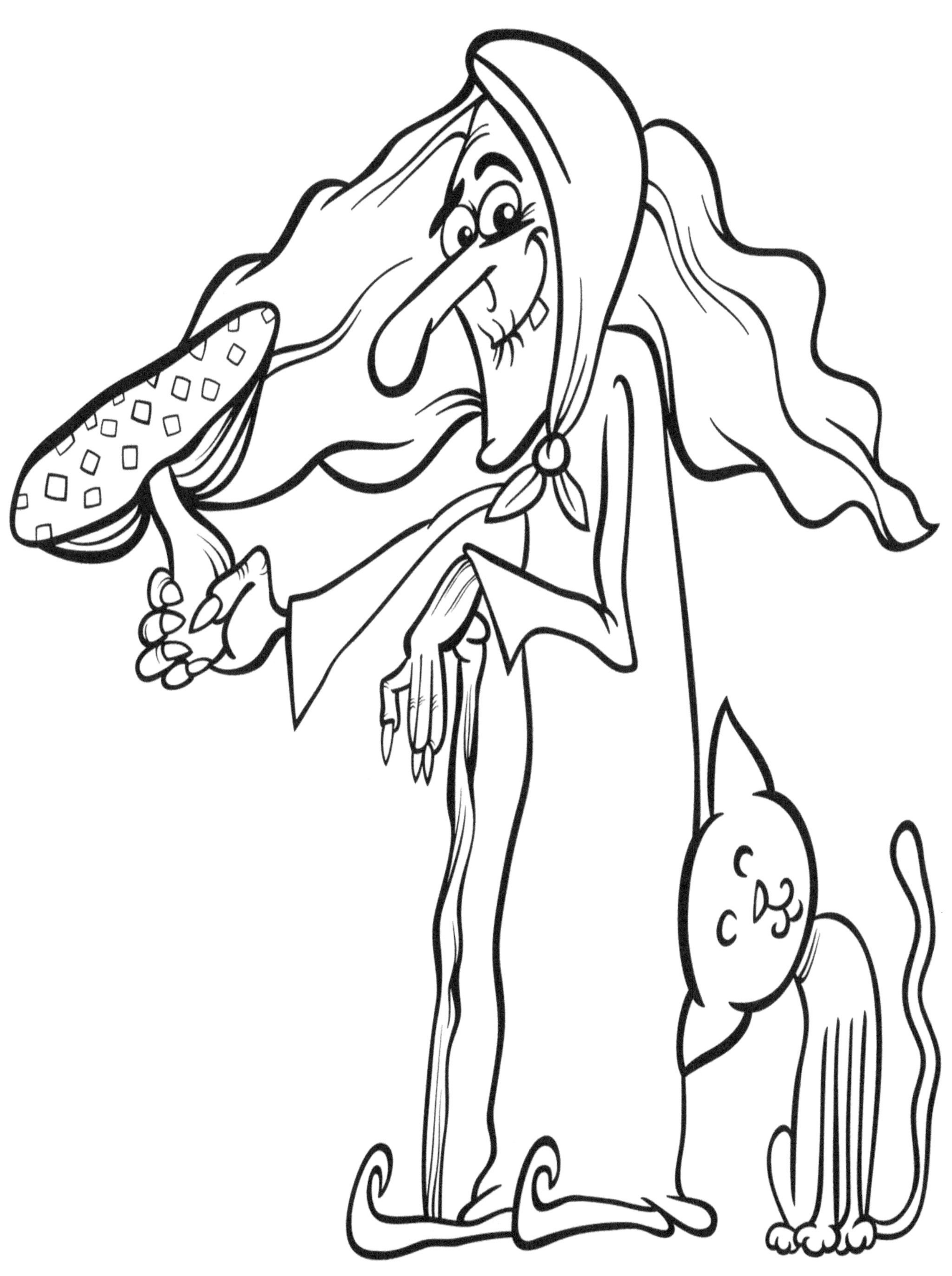

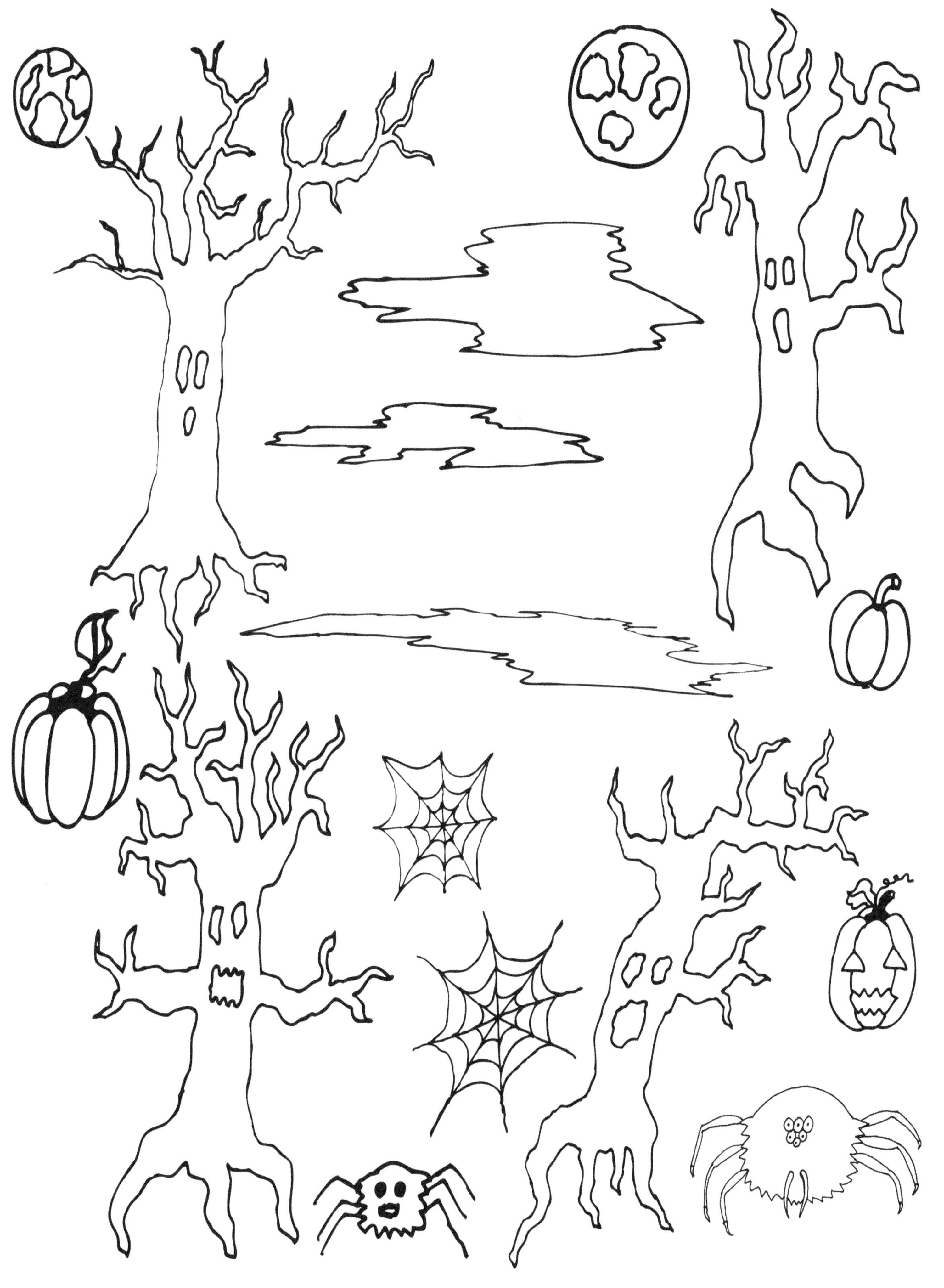

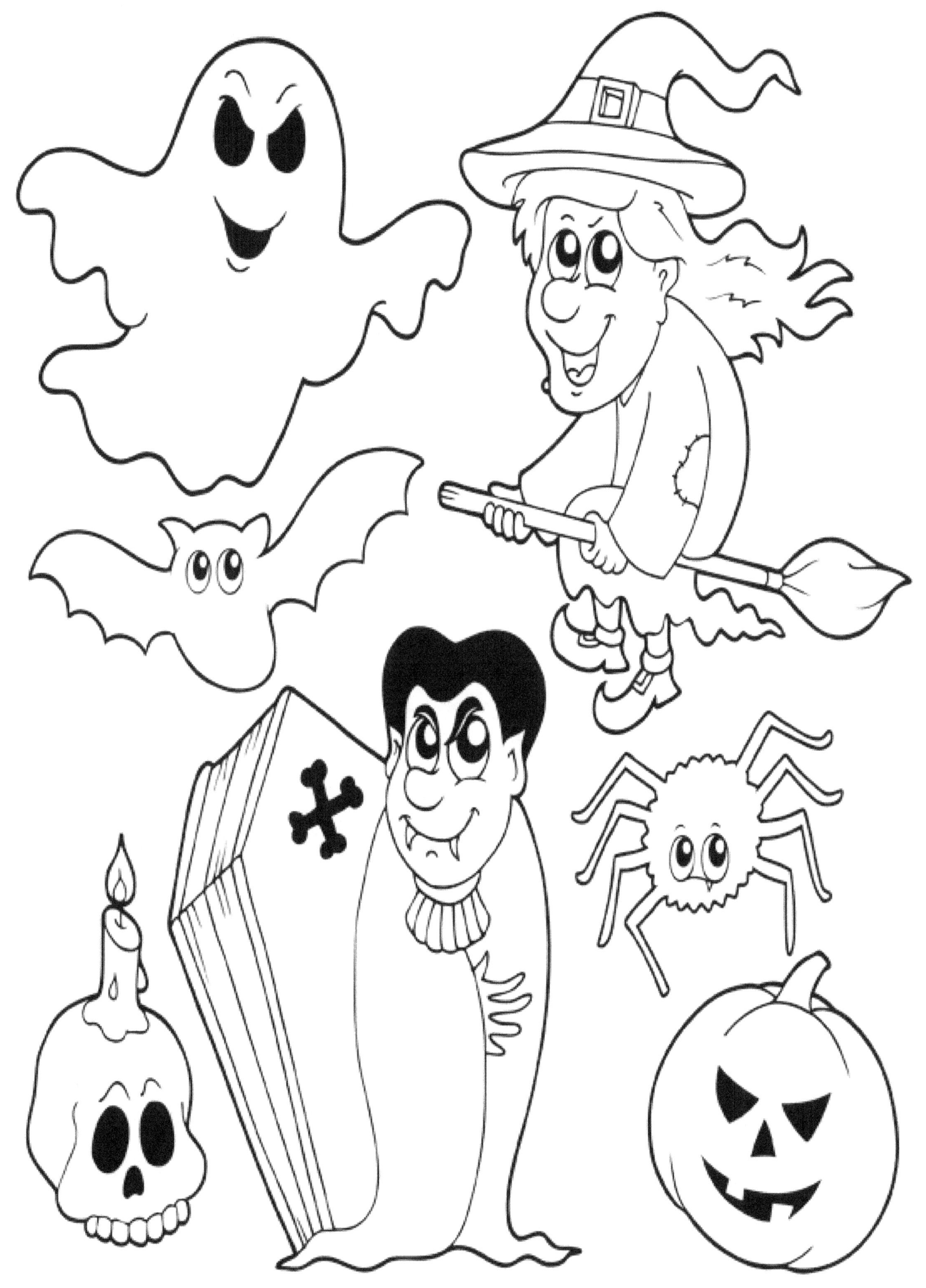

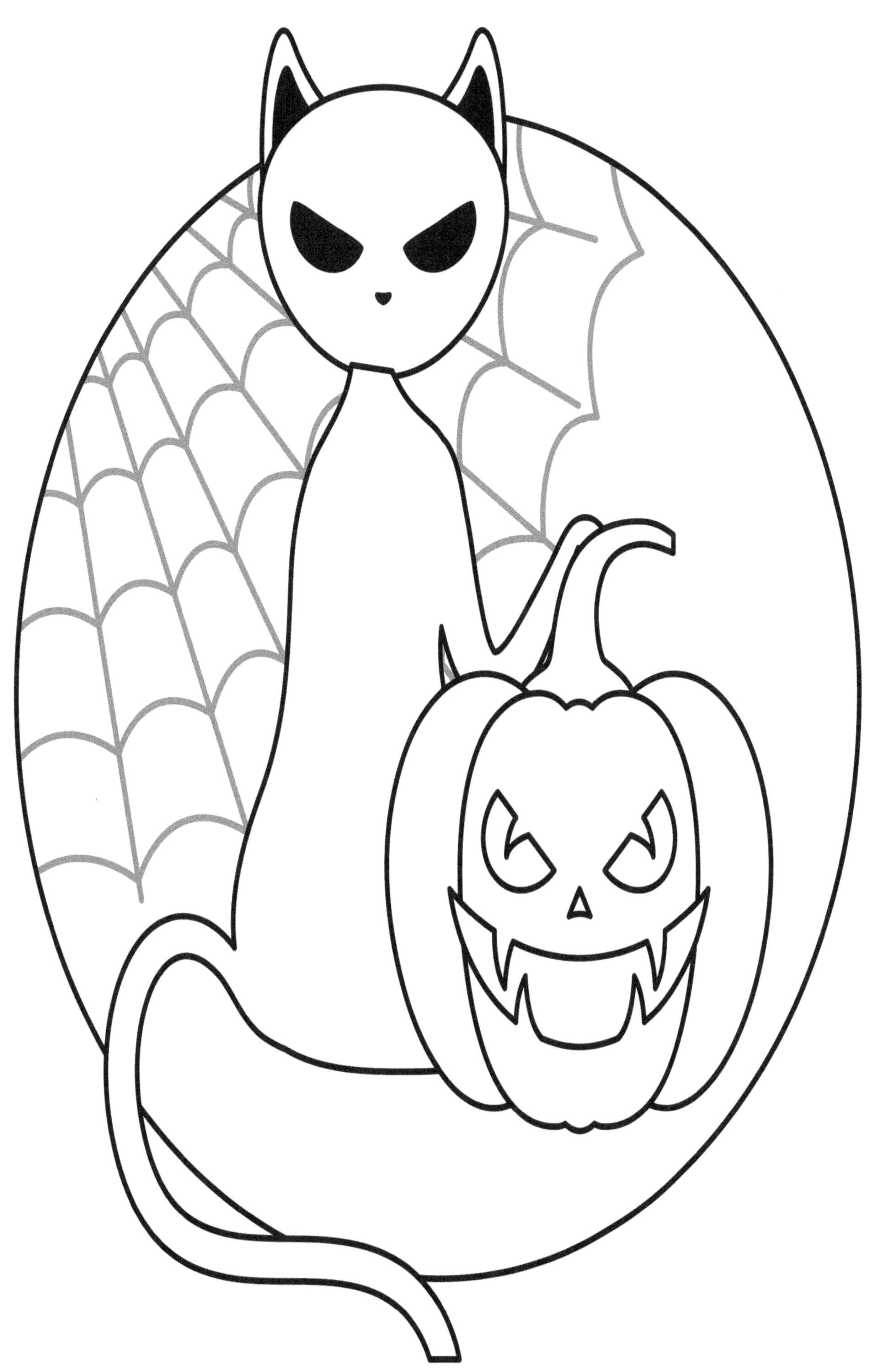

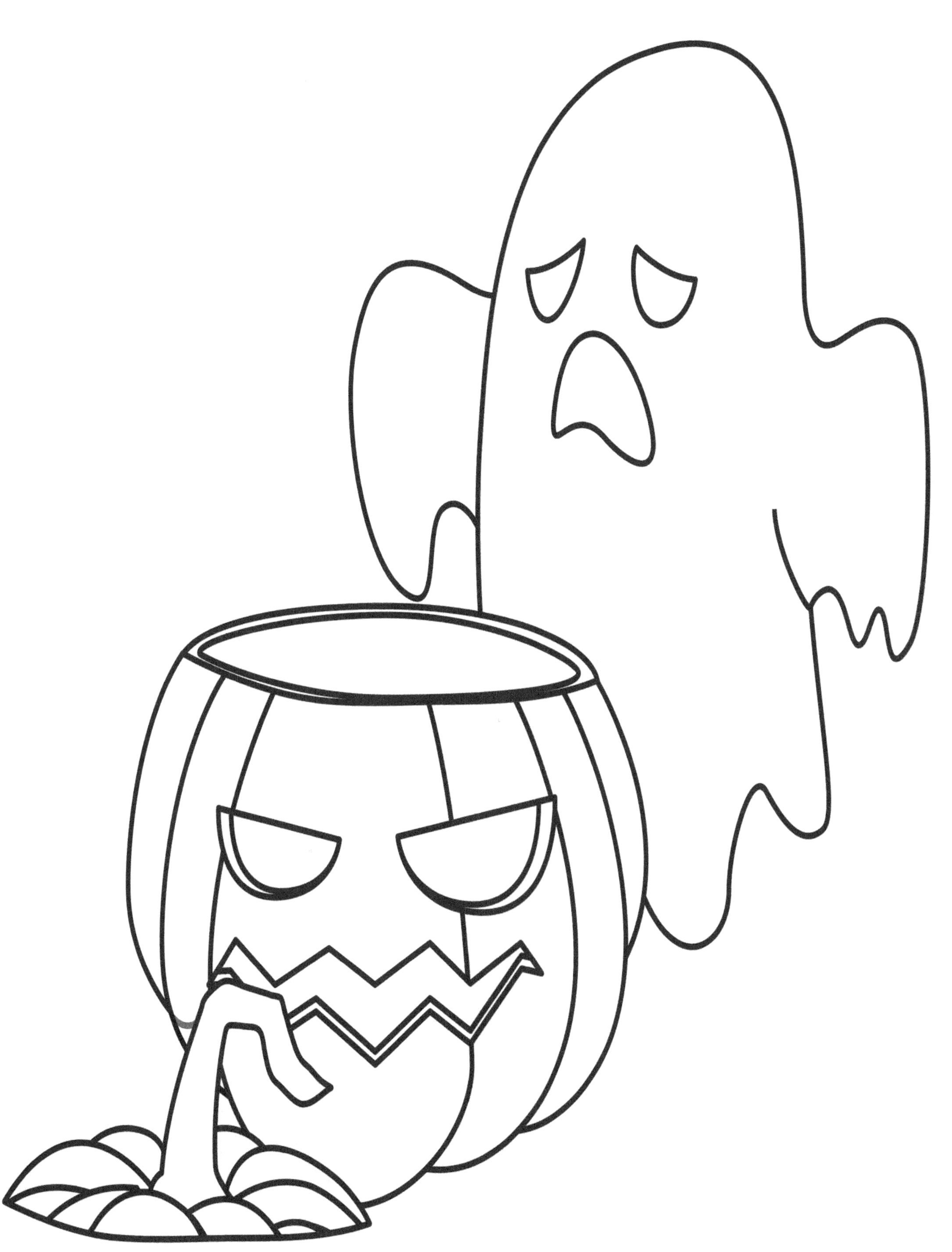

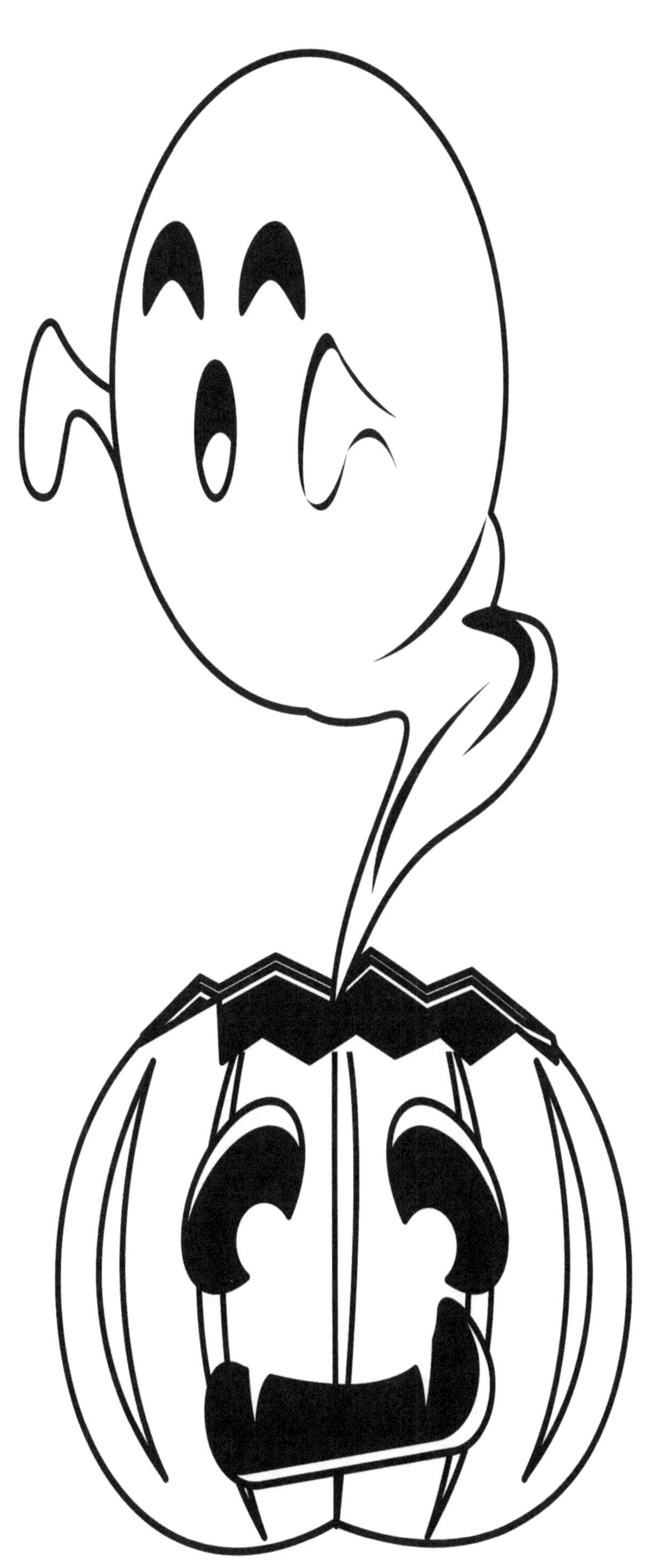

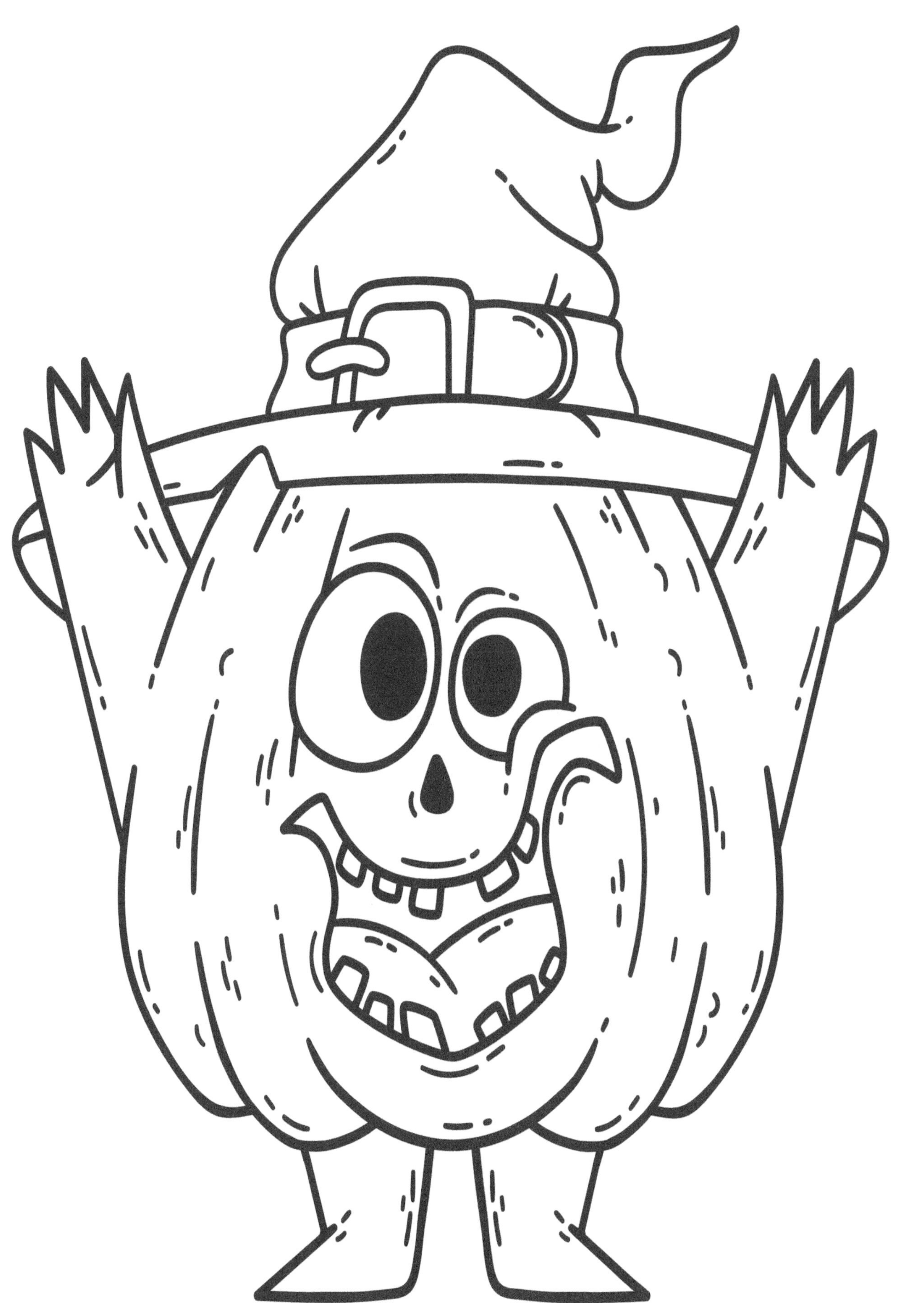

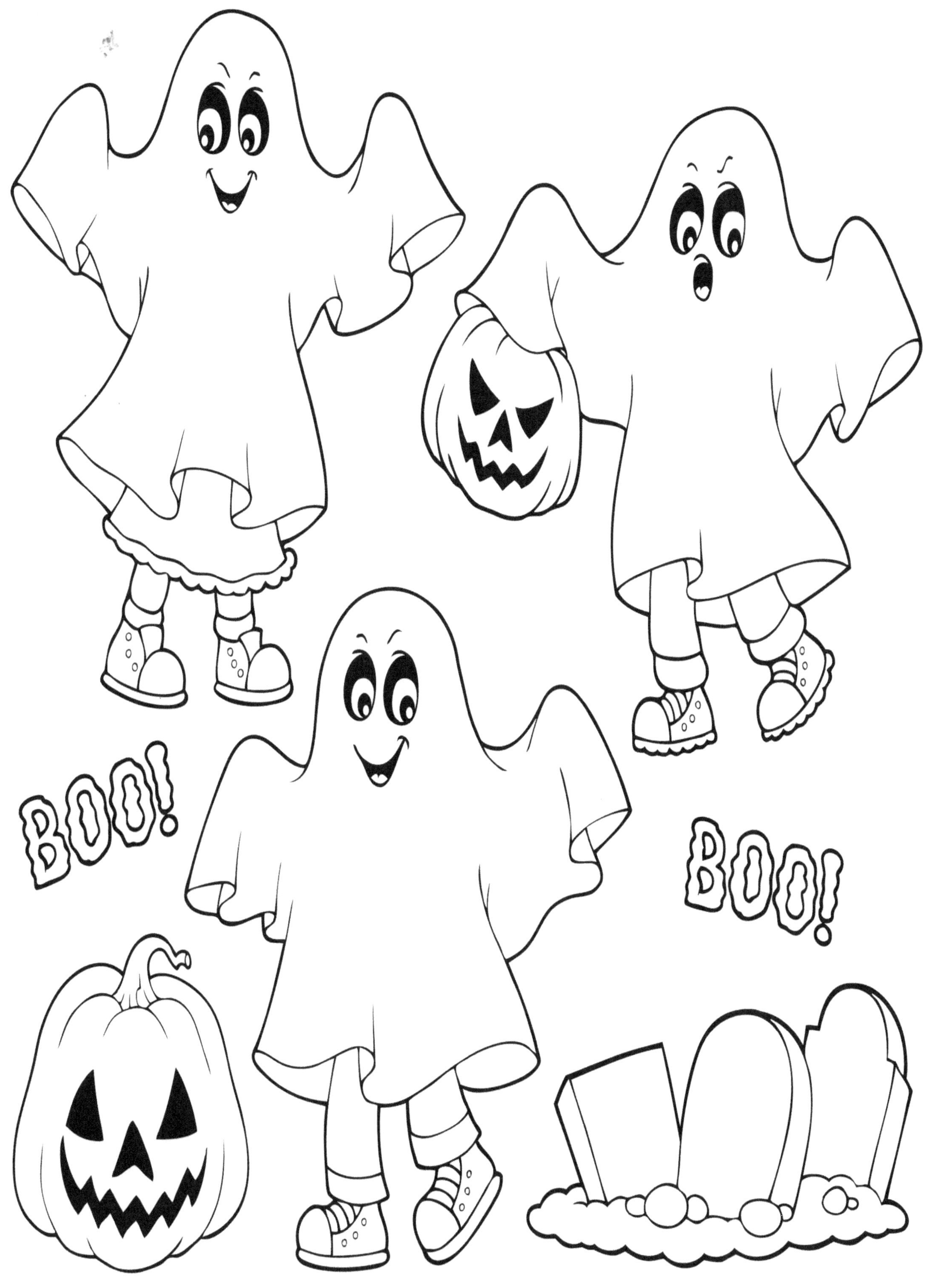

BOO!
BOO!

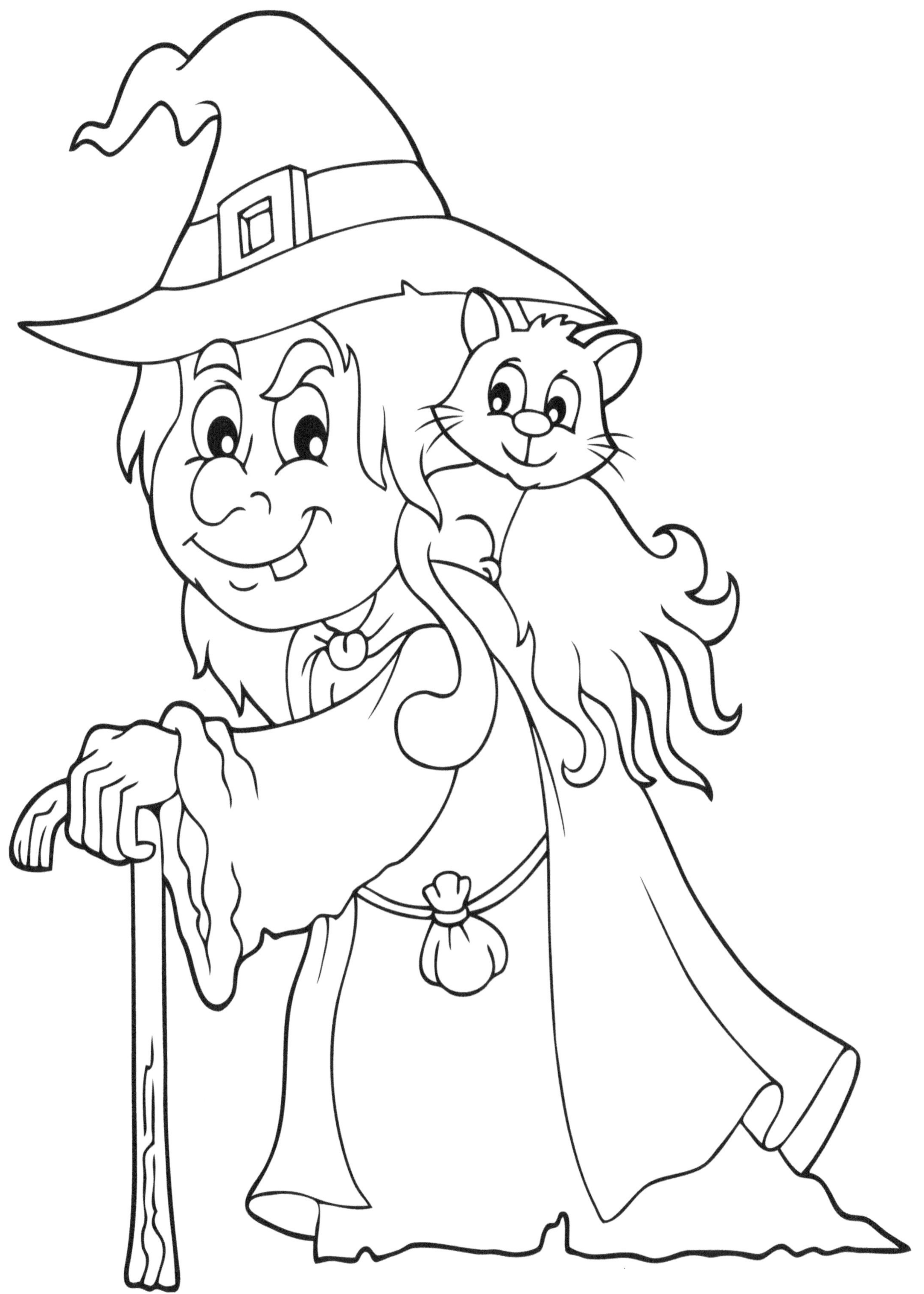

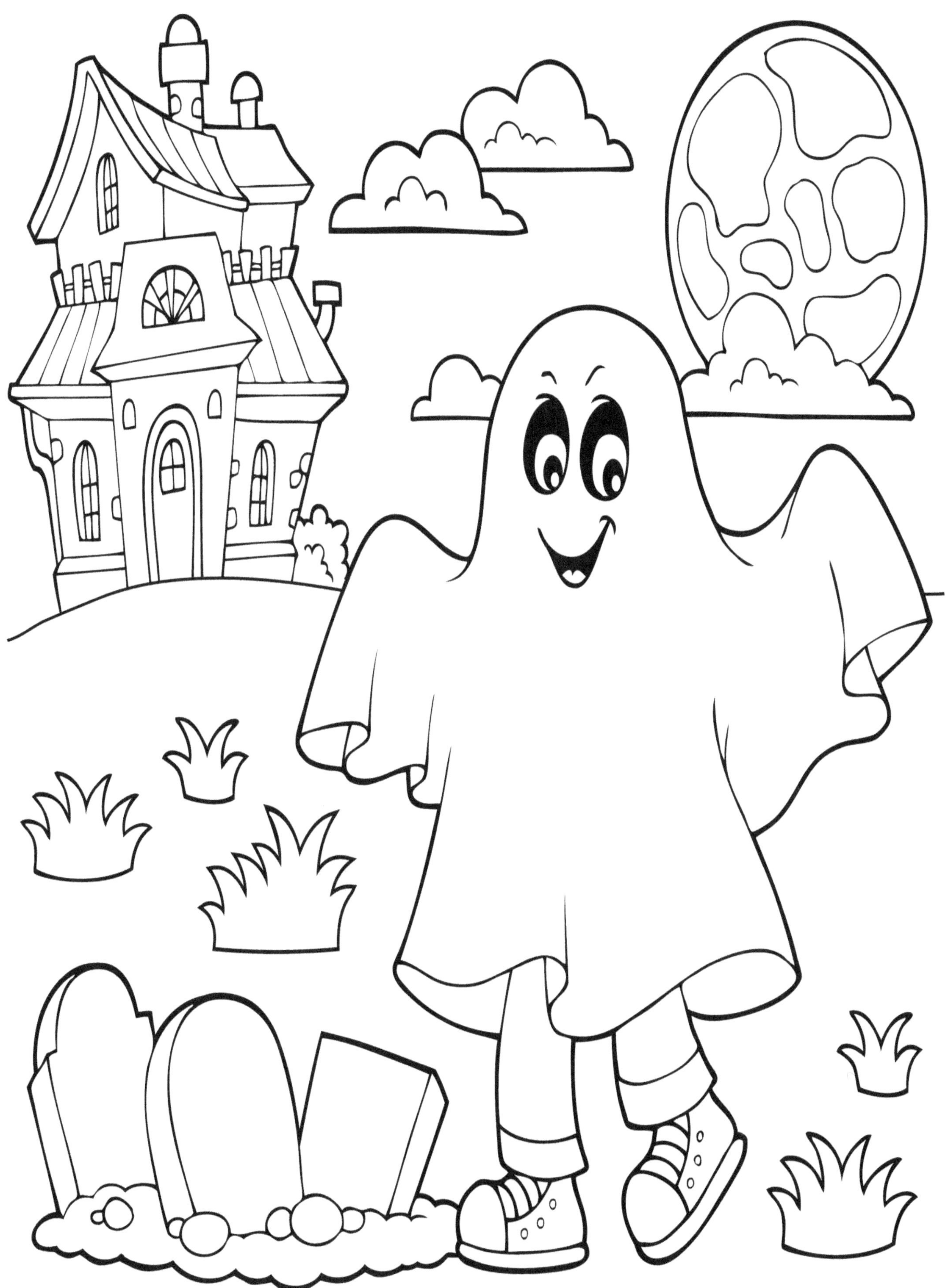

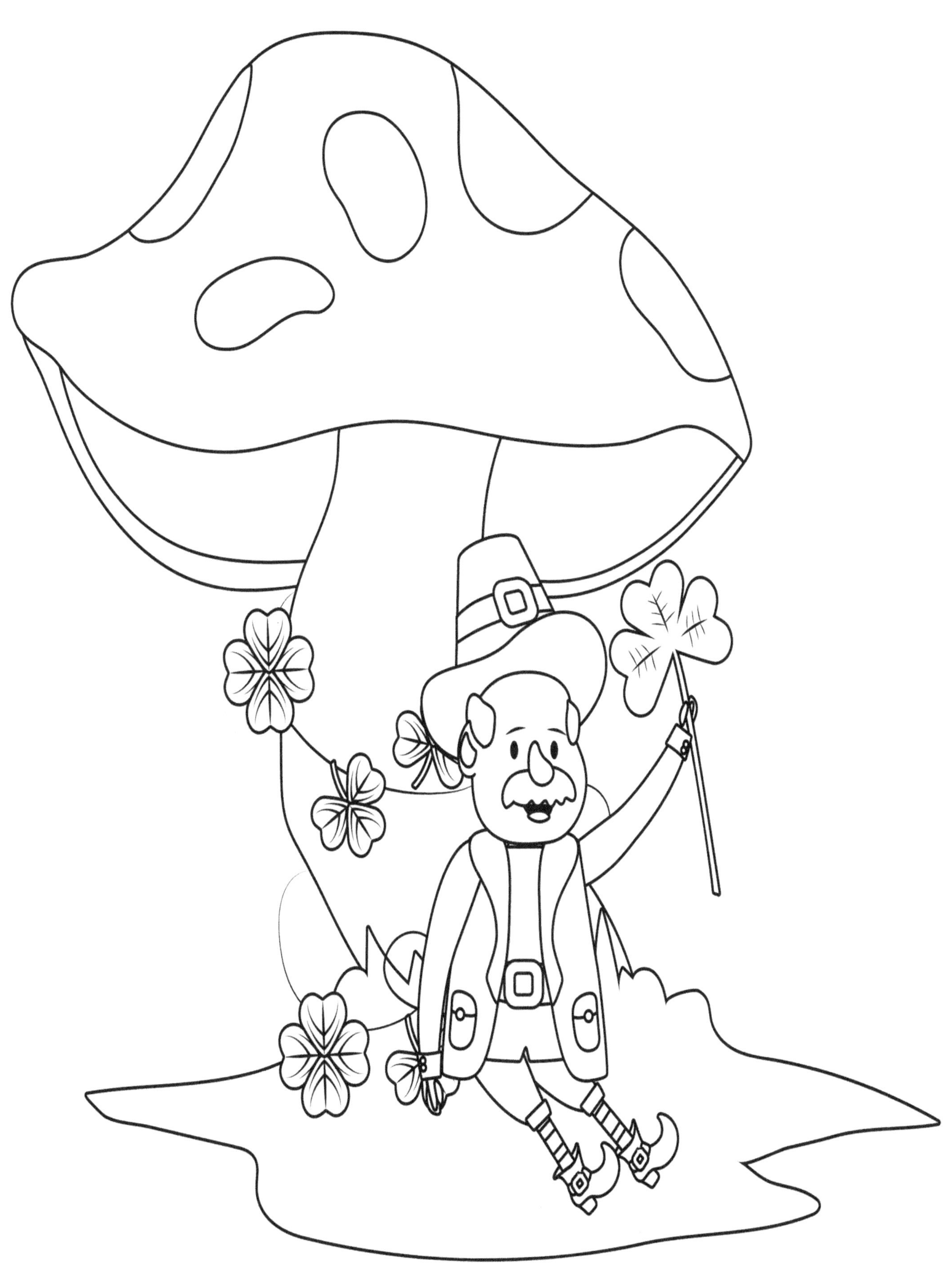

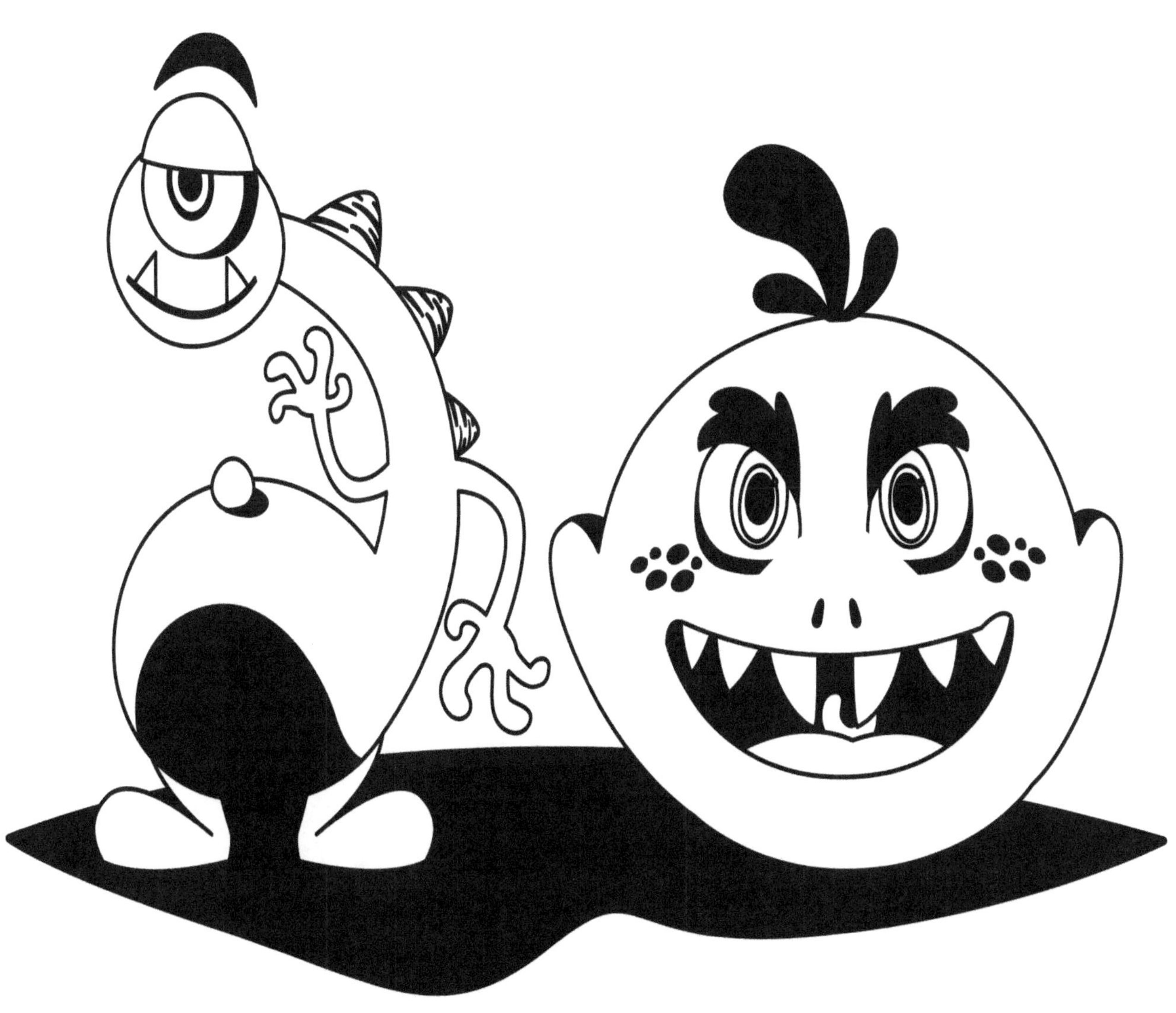